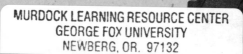

JUST DON'T
DO IT!

JUST DON'T DO IT!
Challenging Assumptions in Business

Joel Brandon

Daniel Morris

McGraw-Hill

New York   San Francisco   Washington, D.C.   Auckland   Bogotá
Caracas   Lisbon   London   Madrid   Mexico City   Milan
Montreal   New Delhi   San Juan   Singapore
Sydney   Tokyo   Toronto

McGraw-Hill

*A Division of The **McGraw·Hill** Companies*

1 2 3 4 5 6 7 8 9 0   DOC/DOC   9 0 2 1 0 9 8 7

ISBN 0-07-043184-1

The sponsoring editor for this book was Susan Barry, the editing supervisor was Fred Dahl, and the production supervisor was Suzanne W. B. Rapcavage. It was set in Fairfield by Inkwell Publishing Services.

Printed and bound by R. R. Donnelley and Sons.

 This book is printed on recycled, acid-free paper containing a minimum of 50% recycled, de-inked fiber.

McGraw-Hill books are available at special quantity discounts to use as premiums and sales promotions, or for use in corporate training programs. For more information, please write to the Director of Special Sales, McGraw-Hill, 11 West 19th Street, New York, NY 10011. Or contact your local bookstore.

CONTENTS

PREFACE

Although there are many very good business schools, thousands of excellent business books, and many business journals, each carrying several brand-new concepts at the time they are published, business somehow remains mysterious. There are very few people in the business world who believe that people of average talents will succeed in business if they just apply what is known as good practice. On the other hand, some fairly untutored people have built large and successful businesses although they apparently lacked any of the wisdom imparted in schools, books, and the best journals. So why should we write another business book, and why should anybody read it? What exactly has a business person to gain in learning new things about business?

Business is basically nothing more than selling something for more than it costs to buy, make, or deliver it—to make a profit. Everyone knows the basics, although remembering them is sometimes difficult in a large organization. We don't need to know more and more about business to reexamine its immutable basis in profit. But large businesses conduct themselves in a way that turns simplicity into complexity. The immediate goal of each and every manager in a company is not the company's profit, but his or her own reward: recognition, remuneration, and the increasingly uncertain goal of retention. Perhaps in the fullness of time, a manager might even hope to be promoted. In reality, managers are not evaluated on profit alone; indeed some are not even in a position to demonstrate their contribution to the company's bottom line. Managers from the very top of the company to the bottom are evaluated not only on what they achieve, but on how they do it, and on what sort of goals they set for themselves. If what they are doing looks sloppy or unambitious, it may actually cause a reduction in shareholder equity, and that will threaten even the CEO's job security.

So a manager's professional life is a constant battle with numbers, and with making educated guesses as to what can be achieved with respect to them. This is where book learning becomes useful. We authors can potentially help managers to reduce the uncertainty of that guesswork. By whatever degree we do that, we make a manager's position more powerful.

Our last book, *Re-engineering Your Business* (McGraw-Hill, New York, 1993), was the first reengineering book published. It helped management to look forward and to reduce the uncertainty that always exists in the area of daily operations: how efficient and effective is the way we do our work? Is operations' contribution to costs as low as it can be—as low as the competition's will be? Reengineering is still a leading edge management tool that has not settled into a cozy spot in management's desk drawers. This book is not forward-looking. In *Just Don't Do It!*, our view is downward. How sure are we of our footing? Are the assumptions we are basing our entire business upon rock-solid, or just a shaky house of cards?

We wrote *Just Don't Do It!* because in our reengineering practice, we have found that invalid assumptions are a real problem in most businesses. They are more often than not the roadblocks that stop progress, the fence that separates cosmetic improvements from substantial breakthroughs. But, in organizing our material, we could see that invalid assumptions are also problems in daily operations management and, significantly, in almost all interpersonal relationships in business. After examining some critical assumptions, most businesses will find that they are standing, if not on a pile of playing cards, then on very soft ground at best.

In these pages, we did not attempt to cover all of the assumptions that a business may make. Unlike our last book, this one is neither a how-to book nor a reference book. It is our expectation that just reading through *Just Don't Do It!* will leave most managers quite able to root out hidden assumptions and challenge them effectively. We hope that this will be your experience.

Many of the assumptions cited in *Just Don't Do It!* are illustrated by brief stories taken from the authors' experiences and from those of close associates. We would like to solicit stories like these from our readers, for future publication. We can be contacted through McGraw-Hill at JSB@annap.inti.net on the Internet.

We would like to acknowledge the help of the colleagues who supplied us with some of the stories in the book, all of whom are credited in the text. Cynthia Brandon was our principal editor and advisor.

Joel Brandon
Daniel Morris

CHALLENGING BUSINESS ASSUMPTIONS

IT IS NOT IGNORANCE THAT IS THE
OBSTACLE TO BUSINESS IMPROVEMENTS,
BUT THE ASSUMPTION OF KNOWLEDGE.

The raw material for dramatic improvement is present in almost all companies. The skill, talent, and determination are there. There are certainly a few slackers and fools in the business world, but not that many. Most business people we have encountered are intelligent, energetic, and thoughtful. We disagree strongly with suggestions that business managers are basically uneducated, cowardly, dishonest, or unfeeling toward their employees. Sometimes managers appear to be all of these things, but appearances can mislead. Many of the factors that make management look bad are well known, but seem to be forgotten when evaluations of business leadership are made:

- **Management has been forced to cut staff** by competitive pressure and by the opinion of stock buyers, who almost always seek a short-term improvement in equity and who reward mass staff cuts by driving stock prices up, while ignoring fulfillment of even less than ambitious business plans.

- **Managers are not permitted by most business cultures to experiment** except in marketing; making a visible mistake is almost always punished in some way.

- **Managers are motivated to act in their own interests,** often against the interests of their businesses, by prevailing *de facto* reward structures.

- **Senior managers are often falsely accused of indecision** when they are given problems with no viable alternatives stated by their businesses' working-level staff, and then are asked for decisions. They are actually being asked to solve problems, not to make decisions, but the accusations persist.

When these problems occur and are not obvious, they sometimes motivate a lower opinion of management than is justified.

If management is so able, why then is business having trouble changing itself to meet the challenges of increasingly intense competition? Why is there an unprecedented level of doubt concerning the ability of business to manage its affairs effectively? There are two reasons: 1) today's managers do not have the tools to do their jobs, and, 2) business today is encumbered with yesterday's baggage. What seems to be a new age of business has so far been not so much a period of rapid change as one of transition from a static business model—one that remains stable between changes—to a dynamic one, in which change will be continual. The manager of tomorrow will have the qualities of today's manager, but will have new attitudes and new tools. The new attitudes are our especial concern in this book.

JUST DON'T DO IT

Today business management is motivated to improve itself, and its company, more than at any time in the past. The question is not whether to change, but how. There is also now more advice about change than ever before. There is so much advice floating around that no manager can possibly learn even half of it. And any manager's opportunities to apply change management methods are equally limited, so today's managers must choose their methods carefully. Each opportunity comes only once, and must result in success.

However, there is always time for one sort of new advice, no matter what approach to change is taken and that is negative advice. In most cases, it doesn't cost anything to avoid doing something: a very cheap addition to a manager's toolkit. It can often work wonders to simply stop doing something.

There are all sorts of bad business practices. Some cannot be discussed in a general management book; they are related to a specific industry, or are even more restricted and apply only to specific companies. Some others are just matters of poor judgment. But there is a class of business problems that can be solved by stopping bad practices, practices that a book can address. Certain bad practices are the result of actions taken in good faith, but based on mistaken assumptions. These assumptions are usually not analyzed on a conscious level. The managers who make them do not realize that these assumptions are the basis of important business decisions. These are the assumptions we are going to challenge.

MANAGING AT A HIGHER LEVEL

Management today is required to operate at a higher level than in the past. Managing at a higher level means setting higher standards for performance and meeting them by managing better. Hence the need for:

- finding better tools,
- using more effective management methods,
- looking at the business operation from new viewpoints (e.g., managing business from a process, as well as an organizational, point of view),
- knowing more of the details of the business operation,
- continually testing and improving the quality of the work being done,
- fine-tuning the capabilities of the workers,
- continually reviewing and testing the requirements and assumptions of the organizational structure, the work, and the human resources for which the manager is responsible.

Competition forces businesses to be better in as many ways as possible: whatever one business neglects, another will use to compete successfully. Managers are forced to gain more direct personal knowledge of the details of their operations than in the past. Managers must take a higher level of control over all business activities, to optimize their results.

To improve their level of control, many business people are going back to the basics and even rediscovering discontinued practices. For example, attention to strategic planning is coming back into favor. Many businesses are reviewing their basic product and marketing assumptions. They are asking "What business are we really in?" or "What business do we really want to be in?" Similarly, process improvement and quality programs (although only recently fashionable), involve going back to the basics of work management. It is also common for information management efforts to review their basic tenets with new skepticism: "What are all of those computers really doing for us?" has been a common question in recent years. The focus of management's attention on basics is part of managing more intensively. It is part of looking everywhere for advantage, even in places that have been reviewed again and again.

An important area in which business is being driven back to basics is that of information technology. As the need for information increases, senior management's trust in information technology seems to be decreasing. Tougher questions are being asked and the basic benefits of computers are being challenged. This is an area in which assumptions are very much in need of examination and often rejection (see Chapter 7, "Information Technology").

CLEARING THE DECKS

Some of the most important reasons to challenge assumptions are related to enabling change, especially to supporting formal change methodologies. To improve any business situation, there are lots of things that can be done, and lots of ways to do them. But before applying any change methodology, why not just stop doing the things that don't work? Clear the decks, so to speak, before taking on a new load.

This does not mean starting with a blank sheet of paper. It does mean that a clear definition of what is impeding progress and causing problems should be undertaken early in any change project.

Today, even successful companies openly state that change is their biggest concern. Clearly, attempts to improve business cannot fully succeed until the cultural and operational abilities to control change are working.

The way to start changing a company is to challenge the basic assumptions and concepts that are simply taken for granted. Managers and workers have inevitably built up a set of assumptions that govern much of their business lives. They do not think about these assumptions, but the assumptions color much of what they do and are actually the foundation for most work styles. Unfortunately, many of these assumptions are as outdated as the concept of a flat earth. Clearing the decks of these false assumptions is the obvious starting point for any future activity—especially for making improvements in the way the company works.

THE ROAD TO SUBSTANTIAL IMPROVEMENTS

If basic assumptions are not challenged, substantial improvements cannot be made. Sooner or later (usually sooner), the progress of any improvement will come up against an assumption and stop. Someone will say, for example, "But we can't ever lose a transaction!" and that's the end of change. Actions that do not challenge basic assumptions are just tinkering at the margins of business.

The essential issue in business is success: How can a level of excellence be achieved and sustained? Making substantial change to achieve a competitive advantage and then sustaining that advantage has been the elusive goal of business in the 90s. While some efforts have succeeded because of creative management, pure pressure, and talent, it seems that as soon as improvements are made, new ones are needed. At the same time, many change efforts have failed. The record of the past five years has been mixed. Why? From our experience, it seems that management has inadvertently arranged for many of its best efforts to fail. The problem has not been lack of commitment, management attention, or vision—as some would have us believe. The problems, more often than not, have been related to flaws in the approach and to the brick walls that are built by unchallenged assumptions.

A large insurance company in southern California engaged a top reengineering firm (not ours, of course) to improve some of its basic business processes. The firm studied a key business process for eight months and drew many charts detailing what the process should be. There was also a very thick report issued. But at the end of the study, the company found that to implement the firm's recommendations, many of its computer systems would have to be rewritten at a prohibitive cost. The firm told the insurance company that the results of the study, and the company's reluctance to implement the recommendations, were due to the lack of complete commitment on the part of the company's senior management. The company thought the consulting firm just did not understand its real problems.

This project was actually condemned to failure from the start because there were assumptions made that were not challenged. The consulting firm assumed that the insurance company would make any systems changes required to implement the recommendations of the project. The insurance company assumed that business processes did not concern the information technology department, and left them out of the study. It would have been easy to challenge both of these assumptions and start the project off on a sound footing. The brick wall, computer systems in this case, could have been avoided or knocked down, if those in charge of the project had known it was there.

EXAMPLE: THE ASSUMPTION OF BUSINESS STABILITY

The assumption of business stability is a good example of one that can destroy improvements before they begin. Although no one in business consciously considers the current environment to be anything but volatile, the unconscious assumption of stability still persists. In making a change, the prevailing view is that one static, unchanging structure that has been used for many years will be changed into another structure that will also last indefinitely. If this assumption was to be discussed before a change project began, it would probably be rejected. Business people fully realize that business must be dynamic and continue to change, as change is required to meet or exceed competitive pressures. However, the assumption is usually not brought to the surface.

The assumption of stability has many negative effects, mostly on change projects. Because of this assumption, the results of a change project are assumed to be permanent improvements in the business. A change that is required to last for many years must be very close to perfect to be acceptable, a condition that sets higher expectations than a change project can achieve. Also, the scope of change projects is pushed up until they exceed feasibility: these projects almost always try to achieve too much. The stability assumption was a key contributor to the well-publicized failures of many change projects in the first half of the 1990s. Handling the sweeping changes that need many years to complete has always been a problem in business.

WHAT ARE BUSINESS ASSUMPTIONS, AND HOW CAN THEY BE CHALLENGED?

We have no new definition for the word "assumption" or for the term "business assumption." The assumptions we will examine in this book will fall into two classes: 1) those that are held unconsciously by some managers in some businesses and may be found either to be true or false when challenged, and 2) those few that are almost always false, and that may be held consciously. The second class can be called "myths," in that they are commonly held and expressed views that are actually not based on fact. For example, one such myth is that business process reengineering should always be started with a blank sheet of paper. It just is not true, but it is ubiquitously quoted as a well-known fact.

Some of the assumptions we have included may seem obvious to many, but they are very much to the point: they are only obvious when they are brought to the surface. Furthermore, some of these apparently obvious assumptions may generally be valid, but pose subtle questions that only conscious deliberation can answer. Almost all of the assumptions in the book are important to consider when attempts are being made to alter the business operation in some way, because they are all part of the inertia of business. Business proceeds on inertia more than on anything else. Once started, a business tends to stay in motion until some catastrophic event threatens. Then it changes, but often much of the change is not properly controlled. Managers involved in change make hundreds of decisions, each of which is based on old assumptions that have become so ingrained that they are seldom, if ever, consciously scrutinized, much less challenged.

Challenging assumptions can be a painful process. Changing beliefs and attitudes is not easy. It also takes time. Even if a new approach is found to be better, the acceptance and integration of the new approach is often fought. But there is really no choice. The basic assumptions of the business must be challenged and changed to provide the flexibility and speed that are needed to survive and excel in the future.

Senior management's job is first to force and then to control this introspection. Conflicting assumptions are common, but they may be debated openly. No one should be given the chance to avoid change by hiding behind any time-honored assumptions, as though they were unassailable bastions. If assumptions are not tested, they may seriously impede any company's progress.

NEW CONCEPTS

While the acceptance of new concepts is not this book's principal objective, there are three presented in discussing assumptions that need an introduction. The first is "Evolutive Management." This term was coined by Professor Stefano Sammadossi, President of the European Consulting Group (ECG) in Milan, where he is also on the faculty of Bocconi University. Evolutive management is characterized by continual change, executed in small, manageable steps that are deliberately taken to achieve a well-planned set of objectives. The word evolutive is intended to have the same meaning as evolutionary, but to be in the active voice, since evolution is something that happens without human control. A more detailed explanation can be found at the end of Chapter 2.

The second new concept, closely related to the first, is evolutive technology deployment (ETD). This concept is a new approach to the use of information technology in business that also causes an evolution in small steps, but that evolves the business's technology. Additionally, this concept incorporates the use of deployment rather than development as the way to provide technology solutions. Deployment, as we use the term, means placing a technology in service, which will generally imply that the technology was bought rather than developed in-house by the business that wants to use it. Today, asset-based technology solutions are sought in place of building systems in-house at astronomical costs, and desktop technologies are gaining an increasing share of the burden of supporting the business over the traditional mainframes. More about ETD is included at the end of Chapter 7.

The third new concept is called value-point analysis, and it is nothing more than an attempt to remove some of the emphasis on pure cost reduction as the sole means of gaining competitive advantage and replacing it with buyer values. The assumption that cost reduction is the only basis for competition is the subject of Chapter 9, in which value-point analysis is discussed.

ABOUT THIS BOOK

In each chapter a set of assumptions about a certain aspect of business is presented. Each assumption is presented with an explanation of what the assumption is and what its impact might be if it is not challenged. Almost all of the assumptions can be valid in some cases and invalid in others. Indeed, some of the assumptions we discuss conflict with one another, so that the same company or person could not possibly hold them both at the same time. For example, some business people assume that computers are great and can solve almost any problem, while others work under the assumption that computers are no good at all, as discussed in Chapter 7. Most of the assumptions discussed in the book are common throughout the business world, but there are certainly no companies that embrace all of them.

Each chapter starts with a brief introduction to the topic, explaining the background of the assumptions related to the area of business covered. The assumptions are presented separately, and are numbered for later reference. Each chapter ends with a summary, a section on challenging the assumptions, and a section on effective approaches to replace the ones that are merely assumed to be correct. In many cases, the points made are supported by short examples. These stories are taken from the authors' consulting experience unless otherwise stated; there are no names mentioned, of course.

The intention of the book is to help managers at all levels to start challenging assumptions. This is not a handbook, and there is no methodology to learn. Just reading the book should give anyone the ability to recognize an unconscious assumption, bring it to the surface, and challenge it. Of course, any assumption that is challenged may, in fact, turn out to be valid. It might be completely valid or just a reasonable basis for action. But if it is not valid, it will probably cause trouble or severely limit management's ability to improve some aspect of the business. It is easy to ignore the existence of unconscious assumptions, or to accept them blindly, challenge nothing, and continue to conduct business as usual. But in today's competitive environment, that approach is business suicide. Just don't do it.

JUST DON'T TOLERATE BUSINESS AS USUAL

CHALLENGING THE ASSUMPTIONS OF GENERAL MANAGEMENT

There are some particularly harmful assumptions that apply to business in general, rather than to any of its specialized areas. This chapter covers these assumptions, that are related to the whole business. Assumptions and myths about business in general arise more easily than those in specific areas because of two problems: (1) the general lack of communication in most businesses, and (2) the increased rate of change that has been common to all organizations in recent years.

Communication problems persist in business even in companies that do their best to eliminate them. Most companies, however, do not make special efforts to communicate. In many companies, senior management even makes a point of keeping secrets. Without certain knowledge about the intentions of senior management, managers and workers throughout the company make assumptions, which in time become hidden assumptions if they are not proven invalid.

Often just making assumptions can lead to their becoming valid. For example, if a rumor is spread that there will be staff cuts, some of the staff (usually the best staff) may leave of their own will, which may cause management to cut headcount ceilings, giving the impression that the rumors were true. Rumors in business that predict specific action have been found by studies to be true in an overwhelming proportion of cases, which gives further credibility to most informal communications.

The following example of communications during a time of staff cuts is typical of such projects, reflecting both sides of the problem: communication not being attempted, and then failing when it is attempted. This example is provided courtesy of Dr. Joan Brandon, an independent organization development consultant based in McKinleyville, California.

> The human resources function in a large West Coast health care organization was targeted to be completely revamped. The project was announced very early in the process, but the process took longer than expected. After one and a half years of redesigning (work that was done by small teams operating without much communication with the working staff), a design was still not ready. Employees had been clamoring all this time to know if they would have jobs in the new structure, but each month they were told, "We will know more in the next four to six weeks." Finally the word came down: all human resources employees were given termination notices but the notices were not dated. They were told that their individual termination dates could be next month, or next year, or maybe never.
>
> The company as a whole also went through restructuring during this time. It is interesting to note that after over a year of mass layoffs, millions of dollars devoted to severance packages and outplacement counseling, and a huge, disruptive effort to redesign all the company's organization structure and work functions, the payroll included over 100 more people than it started with. While no payroll figures were given out, the new positions usually paid more than the ones replaced. So it seems that nothing whatever was saved, and communication from the CEO to the working level was never improved.

A high rate of change in any business feeds its rumor mill, and additionally aggravates the influence of hidden assumptions, simply because of the increasing rate at which decisions are made. Change requires planning decisions, and then even more decisions when the planned changes are implemented, no matter how detailed the plan. Each decision can generate rumors unless the decision is announced openly before anyone can wonder what it will be—a practical impossibility.

Change management as a whole is plagued by invalid assumptions and myths. Several of the assumptions in this chapter apply directly to change management. The basic problem in managing change is not caused by an invalid assumption, but this problem certainly helps create invalid assumptions: in most companies there is little consistency in the ways in which change is managed from project to project. The combination of the natural tendency of change projects to be conducted behind closed doors and their remarkable lack of a consistent management basis leaves most of the company guessing about what they will do next, and of course, assuming the worst.

GENERAL BUSINESS ASSUMPTIONS

Before moving on to an examination of assumptions in specific business areas in Chapters 3 to 9, we will have a detailed look at some of business' general assumptions. Some are very well known, others are perhaps hardly ever brought to the surface. But they can all cause trouble. As with all the assumptions in this book, these are only samples of the possible attitudes and beliefs that need to be challenged. Our purpose is to provide a starting point for an evaluation that will provide opportunities for immediate, cost-effective action. The benefits of meeting these challenges will be obvious in most cases.

ASSUMPTION 2.1
PEOPLE AND BUSINESSES WILL ALMOST ALWAYS ACT IN THEIR OWN BEST INTERESTS.

Few managers or staff consistently place the good of the company above their personal interests (this problem is also discussed in Chapter 5, "The Human Asset.") Whole businesses do not always act in their best interests either. Motivation and success in dealing with controversial issues must always take this fact into account. But, dealing with personal interests is not always easy.

Too often businesses, managers, and staff (at all levels) rely upon the validity of this weak assumption when trying to motivate each other or to forge effective new relationships. Most business people would recognize the risk they were taking if the assumption were brought to a conscious level, but this does not often happen.

The concept of personal interest is not necessarily easy to define. People define their best interests differently based on the situations they face. Trying to anticipate the way people will act should begin with the understanding of what they will believe is in their personal best interest at any given time. This is a hit or miss proposition, because a considerable range of unpredictable factors must be considered, as well as some that are difficult to know. Hate, greed, friendship, and ego are only a few of the factors that can color the definition of best interest. And no one can determine their best interests if they haven't enough information, which is a common case in business today.

So identifying motivating factors is usually a trial and error exercise, at best. However, the need to understand motives is important in most business relationships. Understanding motivating factors is as critical to understanding how to engage the workforce in any planned activity as it is to working with managers. The ability to motivate is just plain basic to getting work done.

The fact is that a company-wide concept of individual best interest cannot be assumed. The things that are important to some are simply not important to others. Unfortunately, without proper motivation, the least important thing to many employees today is the company. This attitude is one of the results of a decade of downsizing, mergers, and layoffs. There is little loyalty and less trust among employees. The belief that the financial, bottom-line view is "the only thing that counts" is at the root of this condition. Few business people associate their personal best interests with those of the company.

We are indebted to Timothy Bremer, a senior independent management consultant based in Louisville, Kentucky, for the following negative example that shows what happened to one manager who actually dared to place his company's interest ahead of his own.

A controller in a medium-sized Midwestern manufacturing company knew that the company was in trouble. He gained this knowledge through his special access to all of the company's confidential financial information. In discussions with other senior managers, he was asked to keep this information confidential and he did so. Clearly it would have been in his personal best interest to leave the company. But he stayed. The company had given him its trust when it promoted him to controller, and he would not desert it. When the company could no longer pay salaries, most of its people left, but he continued to place the company's interests first. When the company went out of business, he was one of the last ones to leave. Afterward, his ability to get another job was hurt by the company's failure, and curiously, by his refusal to pursue his own interests and leave early. His loyalty hurt his immediate financial situation, his job satisfaction, his family, and his career.

Assumption 2.2
In our company, senior management avoids
decisions.

As we mentioned in Chapter 1, many working level staff and middle mangers accuse their senior management of avoiding decisions. This is sometimes true, but more often it is not. As we've noted, senior management is often asked not for a decision, but for solutions. That is hardly the same animal.

We have heard many mid-level managers and even vice presidents complain about the remoteness of their management. They believe that problems should be brought to the attention of their senior managers, and they, the juniors, should be told what to do. This is really not asking for a decision: rather it is asking senior management to tell them how to solve the problem.

A better course of action is to bring solutions to management along with the problem. These solutions should be presented as fully developed business cases, with the costs and benefits of each possible solution included, summarized by a recommended course of action. Then the management team can be expected to decide on the alternative they consider best for the company, in terms not only of outcome but also of feasibility.

Conversely, in many companies senior management cannot let go of the details and they do not like to allow junior-level managers to take responsibility for problem resolution or direction. Delegation is the foundation of empowerment. When problem resolution is not vested in those managers closest to the problem, solutions are often overly complex and may cause even more trouble. Obviously, there are many negative ramifications when management chooses to consolidate decision authority, but it happens in many companies. In these companies no one needs to worry about management making decisions: no one else but senior management is allowed to do so.

In companies where management actually does refuse to make decisions, destructive game playing can often be found. This is a game of testing and revision, played between executives and line managers. The first-level managers try to find out what senior management really wants: the juniors try their ideas and observe the reactions of senior management. Where this game is played, the working levels are permeated with fear and doubt. Mid-level management and even some upper-level managers feel powerless and frustrated. In these companies we often find that the senior managers are equally frustrated with lower-level managers, regarding them as unable to solve their own problems. These situations do not often improve unless they are directly and aggressively confronted. If they are not corrected, the chasm between senior and mid-level management will grow, destroying confidence on both sides.

Where this problem exists, the assumptions of both senior management and mid-level management should be examined. This will usually lead to the beginning of effective role definition and responsibility assignment. If management's roles are not specifically defined, empowerment is only a word, and any empowerment program is a waste of effort.

The establishment of a process of solution recommendation and decision resolution is another important step toward improvement. In most companies this communication just doesn't go on. Everyone assumes that the *status quo* is acceptable, and thus many people operate with unnecessary restrictions. Where this assumption is accepted, the operation is clearly dysfunctional. To improve the effectiveness of the company, this assumption, whether implicit or explicit, should be questioned.

ASSUMPTION 2.3
THE BUSINESS GETS BETTER AND BETTER.

In any business that is not visibly failing, it is common to assume that one's company is improving every day. All companies are occupied with many improvement projects, and the natural course of management is to improve, as is evidenced by the higher goals that every business sets for itself. But the assumption of actual improvement is very often invalid. Actually, business naturally evolves toward mediocrity. Inertia carries many companies through the day and year. Performance is merely checked against numbers, with little attention to the real health of company, the capabilities if its employees, the quality of the corporate culture, or the overall level of teamwork. Teamwork and quality are too often only slogans. Change, planned and unplanned, piles on top of change, and the business loses control over its direction without realizing it. Over a long time, this apparently improving evolution actually weakens the processes that run the company's business. This is retrograde evolution: toward mediocrity and often worse.

On the other hand, informal change at the lower levels occurs constantly, and the business is not really controlled there either. The financials of the company never show this. Narrowly focused management engineering efforts don't show this sort of detailed change. And small changes in workflow don't show up on organization charts. In fact, aside from low-level process charts, if there are any, there is nothing to show that these changes ever take place.

Because process charts are not widely used (and when they are used, they are generally allowed to lapse out of date) businesses of all sizes are typically out of touch with this problem. What is visible, however, is the impact on the budget: the operation takes more money and the staff does less work over more time. Budgets and staffing levels are forced to increase as temporary "fixes" that become permanent and other forms of ineffectual activity cause a sort of operational thrashing. But this is not seen as an efficiency issue. It is not seen as a financial issue. It is not seen as a staffing issue. In fact, most attempts at staff reduction (and other cost control projects) have failed to notice this creep toward mediocrity at all.

In far too many businesses, a principal culprit in the slide to mediocrity is the information technology function. In a majority of companies computer support does not really improve all that much, and systems maintenance causes increasing instability and difficulty in making further modifications to systems. The resulting hodgepodge of information technology services is often ineffective, and the ability of the information services group to support the business is questionable. This deterioration of support is predictable and inevitable in many companies. The result of this problem is an inability to change systems quickly. In most companies the information technology group cannot come close to being responsive: the backlog of activity is just too great and the probability of a change causing other problems is just too high to move quickly. The bottom line is that just as business changes weaken the structure of the operation, systems changes weaken the ability of the information technology group to provide fast, consistent support.

The most interesting aspect of this assumption is that any manager or group will take exception to it for their own operation. Others may have this problem, but not they. For example, many information technology managers believe they are doing a good job and providing high-quality support. The user who must wait long periods to get support and who must deal with surprise system problems disagrees. This example is repeated throughout the company. Sales believes it is fine, but order processing is a problem. Order processing believes it is in good shape, but order fulfillment is a problem. And on and on.

This issue can only be considered once the real nature of change is accepted. The other requirement is that defensive behavior be discouraged. The first of these requirements is perceptional and can be achieved. The second, promoted by W. Edwards Deming and others, is still not being accepted: culture is the most difficult part of a company to change. Even where the financial indicators show improvement and the staff has been cut, this problem exists. Temporary measures will not last long and the problem will rebound quickly.

Unfortunately, this assumption is often overlooked as soon as some indicators show improvements, or as the company just learns to live with its negative factors. This does not necessarily mean that the operation is improving. It probably just means that management is being told what it wants to hear. Finding the truth begins with challenging this assumption.

ASSUMPTION 2.4
BUSINESS IS FRAGILE. IF A NEW STRATEGY IS IMPLEMENTED, IT MAY CAUSE IRREPARABLE HARM. IN DOUBT, THE SAFEST COURSE IS TO DO NOTHING OR TO WAIT.

Today, standing pat is a good way to guarantee problems. If the business is not doing well, it will do worse, and if it is doing well, there will be competitive pressures from somewhere. We are indebted to Dr. Stefano Sammadossi of the European Consulting Group (ECG) of Milan, Italy for the following story, including, in this case, the name of the company.

Pharma Company was a mid-sized Italian corporation. During the early nineties, Pharma Company showed remarkable growth, with revenues increasing at 25 percent a year. The reason was that their research laboratories had developed a new product that was stunningly successful. In 1994, 80 percent of their revenues came from that product. The company focused on just one national market. As it had grown quickly, senior management was not able to expand its thinking beyond national borders.

In 1995, the Italian government's pharmaceutical budget was cut. As a result, sales of the product were expected to drop by 50 percent. Senior management was not ready to face those difficulties; everything had always been all right. However, it was soon obvious that outside help was needed. With the support of a leading consulting company, the company's principal business processes were analyzed.

The main outcomes of this analysis were:

1. Senior management was made aware that it had underrated the company's dependence upon a single product sold in only one market.

2. Senior management was made aware that it had not been able to assess the change in the environment.

3. It was clearly stated that economic growth had hidden the real problems of Pharma Company.

The process analysis looked at Pharma as three independent functional areas: (1) research and development, (2) production, and (3) sales. There was almost no coordination among them. During the last years, most of R&D department employees' time was spent in applied research. This was done on the unquestioned assumption that Pharma Company had to exploit its main product. Consequently, there were no resources assigned to find new products. Basic research was only residual. As a result, no other products were developed, and time and money were wasted.

The sales force was one of the factors behind Pharma Company's initial success. Vendors understood the potential of the product and sold it aggressively. At the top of their growth curve, they got a new contract, with a minimum commission guaranteed based on the prior year's sales. In fact, senior management believed that Pharma Company's growth would have lasted indefinitely, were it not for the governmental budget reduction. When sales dropped, the sales force become nothing but a huge fixed cost.

As a result of lost sales, 30 percent of the workforce had to be laid off in a few months. It was not over. Pharma Company senior managers were not able to react quickly. They had not realized yet what was going to happen; they couldn't believe what they were told. The results of the process analysis lay on their desks.

Because of their "decision-making paralysis," Pharma Company went bankrupt in less than a year. One-half of their sales could have sustained the company if more resolute action had been taken, but this company chose to go out of business instead.

ASSUMPTION 2.5
NOTHING REALLY GETS DONE—NO ONE WILL NOTICE
WHETHER I DO A GOOD JOB OR NOT.

This is the assumption of "lip service managers" and their like among the operations staff, who are always behind in their work. This assumption is, unfortunately, prevalent in business and is found in almost every company. While the reasons are varied, many managers operate under this assumption. When questioned, managers who hold this assumption most often cite the following reasons for their inaction:

- "Why should I even start this project? This is the fourth boss we've had in the last year and he will probably not last long enough for us to finish it."
- "There will never be consensus on this issue, so let's just pretend to go along with it. We will look cooperative but we never need to do anything."
- "This is the third time they've tried this new approach. It has never worked and it will never work. If we are given anything new to do, we can just claim that we had too much work to do, and no one will blame us—after all, the current operation comes first."

Lip service managers live for meetings. They are part of everything that is talked about, but never have time to do anything. Their people are always too busy and when forced to agree to do something they never seem to get it done. While the excuses may individually sound reasonable, their nonproductive trend is clear if one looks for it.

There may be other motivations behind lip service managers, such as fear and just plain laziness. Problems of this sort appear to be caused solely by these managers themselves. They feel that if they don't do anything, they cannot be accused of doing anything wrong. They may also feel that if they look busy and continually carp about being overcommitted, they may duck further responsibility and work. This course of action may actually get more people assigned to them, and having more people may even result in increased compensation eventually.

But is this sort of manager really responsible for the inactivity that he or she produces? No, the real problem is not the manager or staff member who pretends to commit and never produces. The actual problem is the culture that allows this unproductive practice. Some people assume this attitude is acceptable unless they are clearly shown it is not. This attitude is learned. It is only found where managers are allowed to get away with it. Unfortunately, pockets of it seem to be ubiquitous.

This attitude is also a problem in self-managed teams and in empowered teams. In theory this attitude will eventually be brought to light and then not tolerated by team members. True in theory. But the disruption this weeding out process produces is a serious threat to the success of the teams.

A senior manager at a large insurance company managed almost 2,000 people. Of course, there were several levels of managers and then the workers. The senior vice president wanted to cut the budget and improve the operation. Investigation provided many opportunities for quick improvements. The improvements were initiated, with tests to prove that each improvement was viable and also to determine the disruption that each change would cause. The test results were very positive. The projected results were very much worth the investment. The senior vice president wanted to move on the opportunities right away. After several weeks of inaction, the senior vice president called a meeting of the senior manager and the team that designed the changes and asked about the status of the project. The response was that nothing had been done because all the people were too busy. The senior VP again ordered the work to be done as soon as possible and the manager in charge of the area agreed. Weeks again went by and still there was no apparent progress. Again a status meeting produced the excuse that they were too busy. The senior vice president remained kindly and patient and again ordered the work to begin. The senior manager continued to commit herself to do the work, and then continued to ignore the commitment. She was allowed to get away with it—until both she and the senior vice president were fired.

Assumption 2.6
Quality is not my problem; no one has ever mentioned any problem with my department.

Most management is quick to respond to quality problems identified by customers. However, by the time a customer finds a problem, it is very difficult to fix it, and often customers do not report difficulties. They just go to the competition. Management has a source of constructive criticism that could be very helpful if it were used: other departments in the manager's own company. Unfortunately, the views of other departments are usually ignored.

Most managers are motivated through corporate incentive structures to operate without regard for any part of the organization but their own. They might as well actually wear blinders or work in silos (which have become common metaphors for this problem). It is not their fault; this is a pervasive corporate cultural issue. Even when special work groups are implemented to improve teamwork, the team members are likely to bring their own interests with them. This obstacle is a result of a disconnection between the production operation and the human resources function. This interdepartmental contention has its roots in corporate hiring and incentive programs, which still follow the classical model in most companies. People are not rated on their team performance, just on the same old individual criteria stated in their job descriptions and annual plans. So, as new business approaches are tried, many managers are not motivated to make them work. In fact, in many cases the success of the new attempt will hurt the people involved. The obvious result is that the barriers between organizations and managers remain.

There are two sorts of corporate structure common today: strategic business area structure, and functional structure. Strategic business areas, which organize the business around products or customers, are particularly vulnerable to becoming what are known in business as "silos," a term used to give the impression of tall structures built of concrete and therefore impenetrable. Silos do not communicate with one another, and they do not practice any form of cross-functional integration. The silo corporate structure and the traditional methods for evaluation of managerial performance often combine to form a very rigid sort of organizational isolation in business. Managers in these companies are each islands of work. They care only about their own operations and their own successes.

Some senior managers support managerial isolation. They believe that if every manager makes his or her own operation successful, the company will work well as a whole. Some senior managers go so far as to encourage competition among their managers. This approach cannot work even in theory, and has been thoroughly discredited in practice. Isolation builds walls and forces staff to remain within them. In time many people become very protective of their walled kingdoms and stop caring about activity outside their walls. The relationships between these silo organization kingdoms becomes similar to feudal nobles and their estates. Business people tend to align with their silos, and a sort of outlook inbreeding occurs. This is usually not based on shared values, but on something akin to tribal association among the workers. They work together, socialize together, form friendships, and even enter sports competitions as organization-based teams.

Because silo relationships seem to promote morale, cohesiveness, and trust, they have often been encouraged by management in the past. However, they also strengthen "us vs. them" attitudes, internal jealousies, and lack of cross-organizational cooperation, all of which are too common (and very debilitating) problems. Silos themselves are coming to be recognized as serious organizational problems throughout large businesses.

This unhealthy organizational environment causes introspective, self-centered thinking in most of its management corps. In most companies, managers simply do not care what happens in any other department, except as it may affect their own. This also applies to the working levels. Anyone in business who is not evaluated with respect to a given criterion doesn't care about it. If they are not affected by a problem, it doesn't exist. If it is not in their silo, it might as well be on another planet. The competition is more important to most people in business than are their colleagues in other departments. Small companies, and new ones, are obviously less infected with silo disease than large, older ones. Silos thrive on time and size.

Many companies have tried to use cross-functional self-directed teams (called "high-performing" teams) to break this mold. But these teams often become little silos themselves. Silos are tough problems. Moving the corporate culture away from silos and other forms of group isolation almost always requires extensive efforts led personally by the CEO.

Quality, customer service, and the general success of a business affect everyone in the business. Certainly no business person disagrees with this view in the long term. However, in any corporation with isolationist organizations, and in those with high turnover rates and low levels of loyalty, this assumption is often being made unconsciously. When managers are given reason to discard their concern for the company, this assumption becomes pervasive and the company may become dysfunctional. Interdepartmental cooperation and respect for the views of others are the effective ways to challenge the assumption. There is no better view of a business organization than an external view.

ASSUMPTION 2.7
PROCESS IMPROVEMENT IS JUST ANOTHER FAD.

Many managers today see no advantage in using process management of any sort. They manage the business by the financial statement and organization chart, and are satisfied with these tools. But these tools are not enough in today's competitive business climate.

Clearly, the flexibility and speed of change required today call for a different set of concepts and tools. But many of these concepts are new and require experimentation before they can become effective in a company. Many see this as just another fad. We hear:

> "We lived through the efficiency fad and the quality fad, now we will live through the process fad. We were theory X'd and theory Y'd. We were made to feel 'warm and fuzzy' and we were empowered. They have all come and gone. Process will take its turn and fade into the background, just as the others all have."

Is process just a fad? Or is it a new tool that needs internal experimentation to be properly understood and integrated into the decision tools of the company? We have found that process is an important component of business, and process improvement is as necessary to running a business as improving organization structure and augmenting core competencies.

Process itself is a concept long missing in the understanding of how a business operation works, especially service and administrative operations. Manufacturing operations managers generally have a much better grasp of processes than service managers do. In administrative areas, even the Japanese admit to weakness in process management. Without an understanding of process it is very unlikely that an operation can be made more effective. These terms are easily confused: efficiency means that the same work is done for less expense, and effectiveness means that the same goals are achieved, but the work done is more suited to the goal, so the product is not only produced for less expense, it is most likely done in less time and the product is of better quality. Process, the step-by-step method by which work is done, is what determines quality and speed. Process adds value. Process is where waste can be reduced. Management attention to process can improve every aspect of a business' products and services.

Clearly, any real use of process improvement as a management tool requires a change in managers' viewpoints. Process improvement is inherently cross-functional; it represents a slice across the organization's silos. It incorporates a new way of looking at costs and benefits. For many reasons, process improvement projects require the formation of coalition teams and cross-organizational management relationships. These factors go directly against the grain of most corporate cultures, and so actually help managers to overcome long-standing cultural roadblocks.

The use of process analysis and design has opened new ways to look at the operation, and has also introduced new methods to control change. But process improvement is not a panacea. There are certainly aspects of business that are not related to process. Furthermore, like any new tool, process management can be expected to have a rocky start when first introduced. But it has proved its worth, and it is mature enough to be relied upon if it is applied sensibly. Used correctly, process management is providing solutions to tough problems, such as the one in this example that dates to the late 1980s:

A Fortune 500 publishing company in the Chicago area had a problem with order fulfillment. Among their principal products is a reference library of very time-critical information. This library is sold in industry (finance, mining, aerospace, agriculture, etc.) groupings. The objective of their sales effort was to encourage customers to move from a lower-level grouping to a higher-level grouping that pertains to more industries. The sales staff had a real problem, though. When a customer purchased a higher-level library, the old order was canceled and a new order placed. This process took up to 90 days. The library updates, which were so time-critical that they came out weekly, were not sent to the customer during this 90-day period. The more the sales force succeeded, the bigger the problem became. The problem was so visible that the competition would literally follow the publisher's sales staff, and offer competing updates on an immediate basis when the customer became disgruntled. The more grouping upgrades the publisher sold, the more business it lost.

The publisher reacted by first scrutinizing the order processing area and then the warehouse operation, using traditional management reviews. They spent a lot of frustrating time assessing these areas. Three consulting groups were called in, one after the other, and all failed. Another consulting group that focused on process was called in. This group began by constructing a model of the entire process. It was found that the process wove its way back and forth through five departments and involved more than 50 people. Management was surprised by the complexity and by the real problems, when they were found. The problems did not occur in order processing or in the warehouse. The problems were found in the interactions among all of the groups responsible for order processing, including the financial groups and the sales group, and also in the way the information technology systems worked. For example, there was a policy implemented and executed by finance that for any order over a given threshold, an exhaustive credit check was required, even for current customers. This process took weeks. Also, in placing a new order for a current customer, no change was allowed to the current subscription. The old order had to be canceled and a new order added. Due to the cycles of deletion and reentry imposed by the computer system, this process also took weeks. Additional time was lost by the sales group mailing its orders into satellite sales offices, were they were logged and forwarded to the order processing department by ordinary mail. The back-end time was clearly not a problem. Once the entire process was understood (and the metrics of each step were defined and numerical data obtained), the problems became clear and the solution was obvious. Changes in order flow, in policy, and in the computer systems were made. The new process took seven days. It could have been done in three: four of the seven days were provided for the sales staff to review the change. Once the process was under control, quality as well as timing could be considered.

ASSUMPTION 2.8
THE CAUTIOUS APPROACH IS BEST, OR SIGNIFICANT PROJECTS MUST BE THOROUGHLY STUDIED.

Caution in all its forms seems a good concept on the surface. It seems reasonable and it has been respected throughout recorded history. Some caution is certainly necessary. The real questions are: "How much caution is good?" and "When is even a little caution disastrous?"

There is good advice on this topic from an unlikely source: poker. An old adage in the game was made popular by the television series *Maverick,* in which Beau Maverick gives the following advice to his sons: "Never draw to an inside straight and never hold a kicker." Holding a kicker is hedging, not discarding a high card when trying to improve on two of a kind. Holding the extra card reduces the odds of improving the important pair into a much more powerful hand. It is the same in business. Once a course of action has been determined to be beneficial, caution reduces the odds of success. The overcautious manager is holding a kicker.

This assumption also takes the form of the maxim: "You must learn to walk before you can run." Evolving in manageable steps is usually a good idea, but taking a step that does not need to be taken at all, out of pure caution, is usually a very serious mistake. It will cause delay and it can cause many other problems as well. We have seen cases where the cautious first step was actually harder to achieve than the final goal. In other cases, the first step was not really a step toward the final goal and did not help in evaluating the more ambitious initiative. There is a place for caution, but it is too easy to apply it everywhere.

Here is an interesting example of a series of cautious maneuvers, each of which seemed reasonable, but that in aggregate were disastrous. The example, with the company name included, is provided by Stefano Sommadossi and Simone Collu, European Consulting Group (ECG), Milano, Italy.

I.M.C. was a leading European mid-size plastic material manufacturer with two lines of business:

1. Design and production of molds and molding equipment.
2. Molding services.

I.M.C.'s customers were very large companies belonging to highly competitive industries, such as personal computers and appliances manufacturing. Therefore, they needed to carry out aggressive cost cutting to survive. Furthermore, the business concentration that took place in the 1990s had created fewer and more powerful customers with increased purchasing leverage. As a result, suppliers' prices had to drop in step with market prices, and I.M.C.'s profits were shrinking continually.

In the past, the company had always been focused internally. Since its market was stable it was able to make high profits. Therefore, I.M.C. senior management was conservative in its vision, and there was no immediate agreement on the need for change. On the other hand, the company's small scale allowed the chairman to shorten the decision-making process: he had the power to do the right thing. As a result, once he realized that I.M.C. had to change its way of running its business, everyone would follow the direction he decided upon.

In 1995, senior management realized that a switch from production to customer orientation was vital to the business' future. The first step for I.M.C. was the assessment of its strategy and processes with the help of a management consulting firm, focusing on business process reengineering.

The aim of the project was to define the company's long-term business strategy and to dramatically improve business process efficiency and effectiveness in order to maintain market leadership. To get started, the project team developed a top-level process model and assessed the current processes, after defining cost drivers and key performance indicators. Three main processes were identified:

Bid making process
> To gather customers' requests, collect technical information, estimate the cost of the project, and issue a bid.

Product industrializing process
> To translate the product design into molds and produce the molds.

Order fulfillment process
> To supply products complying with the terms of customers' orders.

This analysis generated two main guidelines:

1. Integration with main European customers, to acquire competitive advantage and to cut costs. The goal was to break down the traditional barriers between different elements of the supply chain in order to shorten time to market and improve efficiency and profit.
2. Developing new skills to discover new ways to meet customers' needs.

Management began a reengineering effort of the main processes to increase efficiency and performance. The explicit objectives were to reduce the time needed to produce prototypes, to lower production costs, and to assure on-time delivery. Fast response in product industrializing became a priority; scraps had to be reduced from a current level of 15 percent. The reengineering program included interventions in the areas of information systems, human resources, and technology infrastructures. Integration and reengineering projects implied a strong strategic shift. I.M.C. had to move from a long-standing internal focus to a new customer-driven process orientation. The company had to follow its customers, that is to say all global corporations, everywhere.

In general, the company was reluctant to do that. Indeed, the main customer was going to build new factories in Eastern Europe. To follow its customer, therefore, I.M.C. would have to establish a joint venture in the same country, so the joint venture company would be able to set up a facility near its customer's plant.

A specific plan was drawn up to comply with local rules. A feasibility study showed huge benefits and high returns on investment due to guaranteed orders. Nevertheless, too much time was lost. Senior management didn't fully understand that they had a chance to grow faster than they had ever done. I.M.C.'s chairman only saw the risk of cultural shift and chose a slow and cautious approach to change.

He was wrong. It took six months to realize that the company should truly reengineer, but it was too late. In fact, I.M.C.'s main customer chose to integrate with other suppliers. Moreover, the delay in reengineering business processes caused further losses of service level and consequently the loss of some other clients.

The key success factor of the initiative should have been *empowerment*, not caution. Setting up new facilities implied trusting people to foresee customers' needs and to suggest new solutions, but senior management was not ready to loosen its grip.

Analyzing a problem over an excessively long period can also result in an outdated solution. The situation may have been overtaken by events before anything is done about it. As in all business-related affairs, the executive is forced to do the best possible job with the resources available, in this case time. It takes considerable courage to risk the business when there is no certainty of success, but sometimes that is what is required of high office.

ASSUMPTION 2.9
FAILURE IS UNACCEPTABLE.

This is a very common assumption, but there are no businesses that have found a way to consistently avoid failure. Projects fail, new lines of business fail, old lines of business fail, and computer systems fail. It happens every day, and it happens to some very successful companies.

But there are two very different sorts of failure in business. The first is a failure to perform up to reasonable and clearly communicated standards, such as an error in performing daily operations. For example, cutting diamonds is very difficult, but a diamond cutter is not allowed mistakes. The second sort of failure occurs when an experiment is tried and the results are not successful. Despite the obvious differences between them, the two classes of failure are not often considered separately by managers. For this discussion they will be sharply differentiated, and we recommend this to everyone.

Most companies do not readily accept the concept of experimentation (except in marketing). The idea of trying something and getting a big win if it works, but accepting some wasted motion if it does not, is emphatically avoided. It is assumed that management will not tolerate even the appearance of failure. This is too often true. But it does not always reflect the attitude of management, especially enlightened management. For example, Steven Bell of Empire Blue Cross/Blue Shield in New York includes the following admonition in his pep talks when opening change projects, so as to exhort his associates to try new approaches:

> "Don't be afraid to make a mistake. If we are not making an occasional mistake, we aren't trying hard enough."

When management does not take specific steps to assure staff that trial with some error is acceptable, the staff will invariably assume that failure will be punished.

This assumption drives out entrepreneurial spirit and creativity. It promotes a "don't take a chance" culture. This culture will not support success in an age of increased competition. The nimble company of the future will be capable of rapid change, some of which will include trial and error. There just won't be time to be sure of every change, and some changes that can't be guaranteed will have to be attempted for the sake of competitiveness. Many changes will be tried and will fail. But if risk is assessed and controlled as well as possible (by using incremental approaches, for example), the company of the future can evolve through both mistakes and successes quickly and inexpensively, maintaining continuing success.

Also, where the failure of a new approach motivates firing or punishing an employee, management is strongly advised to reconsider. Such a response is destructive and shortsighted. It is frequently seen by the rest of the company as hypocrisy, the failure being used as justification for a personally motivated action. It will always create reluctance to try new approaches and even to be associated with change in any way.

Even when there is a failure to perform, the first class of failure in business, some circumspection is recommended. Of course poor performance is not to be encouraged, but there are many cases of bad results being the outcome of simply trying too hard. Managers obviously want the extra effort from every employee, and want to encourage staff to contend against unfavorable odds. There are also cases in which lack of success is completely unavoidable, the result of factors beyond the control of the workers who may be the apparent targets of blame. Indeed, even when there is a genuine mistake, a manager may want to consider tempering the response so that staff will be quick to report such incidents, rather than compounding the damage by deception.

In summary, challenging this assumption is straightforward: each failure in any business situation ought be analyzed. There are lessons to be learned from all of them. A company that learns from its failures grows stronger. A company that merely punishes failures will repeat them, but in an age of fierce competition, it will not repeat them for long.

Assumption 2.10
Significant change takes a long time.

This assumption is a remnant of the past. No company can afford lengthy projects today. They deny opportunity, absorb resources, and stifle evolution. Lengthy changes take effect too late to remedy the immediate problems of the day. Long change projects have historically high failure rates. They are not needed and cannot be tolerated. But many, perhaps most, managers just assume that significant changes require many months, usually years, and that assumption is very nearly always self-fulfilling.

The reality of business today is that many former constants are now in a state of flux. Change is the norm, and with it has come delay. Delay in change projects is not unusual—it is, in fact, expected—but it must not be accepted. Delay causes real problems. For example, it is not unknown for a change project to take so long that it does not even fit into the business operation by the time it is finally completed. Another common problem associated with lengthy projects is that management must either freeze the operation until a new project can be completed, or risk the operation changing by itself while the project is also trying to change it. The business operation is a moving target, and the longer a change project lasts, the more the operation will move. This problem is becoming more troublesome as the pace of business change continues to increase.

The third problem that this assumption causes is a commitment to the inflexible project management concepts of the past. If the assumption is made that projects will necessarily be lengthy, management will require inflexible, bureaucratic supervision for all change projects. This problem perpetuates itself. Any manager who is unfortunate enough to be assigned a high-profile project clearly does not want to make a mistake. So the old protective methodologies continue to be used. The long time spans that the projects require also delay the day of reckoning upon which projects must show results, another reason there has been little pressure to shorten project life cycles. It must also be said that outside consultants tend to corroborate (and often seek) long project durations, for entirely selfish purposes. So projects continue to take just short of forever.

This is not necessary. There are new approaches that limit exposure and allow projects to move quickly. They are based on the belief that products must be created and deployed in weeks, not months or years. The return on investment using this approach is also likely to be much greater, so that most projects structured this way actually pay for themselves before they are completed.

ASSUMPTION 2.11
CHANGE, HOWEVER NECESSARY, IS A NEGATIVE FORCE.

The assumption that change is bad is subtle and seldom held consciously, but it is very influential. It is also surprisingly common. Many managers see change as a problem rather than as an opportunity. This results in the following problems among others:

1. procrastination in starting needed projects;
2. completely lost opportunities;
3. under-allocation of resources, leading to project failure;
4. failure to accept valuable recommendations arising in change projects;
5. increased costs and waste due to the failure to correct known problems;
6. stagnation and decay of staff skills.

This assumption manifests itself as the unconscious conviction that change should be avoided whenever possible.

No assumption of this sort can stand up to rational scrutiny, so no manager can actually state that change is negative and not expect to be corrected. This is, however, an easy assumption to make unconsciously, especially when there is a choice between changing and not changing. It is common to consider whether or not a situation is really bad enough to require a change. This is not a truly businesslike question. To correct this approach, remember that one advantage that business has over other fields is that decisions can be based purely on bottom-line profit. The most complex factor that need enter into a business decision is how long a horizon to choose when evaluating a proposed change. There is no need to worry about whether or not to make one: if it increases profit, make the change.

ASSUMPTION 2.12
CHANGE SHOULD ALWAYS BE DONE AS CHEAPLY AS POSSIBLE.

This assumption is closely related to the previous one. If change is bad, it should certainly be done as cheaply as possible whenever it is unavoidable. This assumption can also stand alone, and either way it can cause real trouble. To assume that any change project is only an added expense motivates underfunding projects and leaving out anything that looks like it might be optional, practices that have ruined many projects for lack of a small increment of funding. This assumption is what makes change projects the first targets of budget cuts. The reasoning, if it is subjected to conscious deliberation, for cutting change projects is that the business will be no worse off if the change is not made. This is definitely not the case.

A large human resource consulting firm spent several years redesigning and then rebuilding its most important computer systems, systems that directly supported its main line of business. The company spent several million dollars on this process and had already made budget commitments based upon the improvements that the new system was to deliver.

After most of the system had been completed, the computer hardware on which it was to run was ordered. The equipment, desktop workstations, arrived at a bad time for the company, and cash was in short supply. The company's senior managers issued instructions that the boxes containing the workstations were not to be opened, so that they would not have to pay for the new hardware. The equipment cost less than one-tenth of the cost of the overall project, but no benefits could be realized from the investment until the workstations were unpacked. It took six months to get permission to open the boxes. This decision cost the company six months of the benefits of the new system. But the decision was not based on numbers; if the numbers had been worked out fully, the benefit would have been seen to outweigh the costs. The decision was based upon assumptions, in this case invalid ones.

ASSUMPTION 2.13
EVERYONE WHO NEEDS TO BE INVOLVED IN A CHANGE PROJECT WILL BE INVOLVED.

This assumption sneaks into change projects after they begin. No manager would knowingly start a change project without making sure the project is connected in some way with all of the interests in the business that should be involved. However, it often appears that after the project is completed, there were some decisions made without complete participation by some key players, resulting at least in embarrassment and possibly in the total failure of the project.

The groups left out of change projects are often support groups, such as information services and human resources. These areas are either forgotten, left out because they are not thought to be able to contribute, or deliberately left out because they might present obstacles. While support areas are seldom key contributors to business changes, they are often required afterward to supply some key elements that should have been considered earlier. They can be included by some sort of liaison arrangement rather than supplying a full-time team member, but leaving them out altogether is dangerous. In all cases, frequent checks should be made of the project to see if the project's work has gone into areas needing additional contact with other personnel. In Japanese business, a change is always approved by every manager who might be affected by it, in a rather ceremonial fashion. Perhaps a more informal but equally cooperative approach could be of use outside of Japan.

ASSUMPTION 2.14
THERE ARE NO RESOURCES AVAILABLE FOR CHANGE.

This assumption is one of the principal impediments to improvement in many businesses. It has several variations, including:

- the assumption that if resources are used for change, there will be a catastrophic impact upon regular operations;
- the assumption that too much change going on at once would result in chaos; and
- the assumption that there is not enough time to do anything new.

Solving these problems is just a matter of controlling the time and attention of project team members and their management. Many companies (and groups within companies) have overcome all of the difficulties involved in scheduling change projects. They have contrived to change themselves successfully, proving these assumptions invalid. Still the assumptions persist, stopping needed improvement before it starts.

A large eastern insurance company started a series of successful process improvements in one department. Another department became interested and used the same approaches, but the second area ran into roadblocks. One of the roadblocks was the persistent claim by managers that they did not have time to try any experimental workflow, nor even any resources to implement new methods that would clearly reduce effort. The squabbles over resource allocation issues took more time than constructive discussions in the project's weekly meetings. Management's excuse was always the same: no resources, since every resource available was needed for daily work. These objections finally stopped the project.

Two months after the project ended, senior management mandated an across-the-board budget reduction for the entire department of over 20 percent. The reduction was much greater than the amount that would have been reallocated for the change project, with no concomitant reduction in work effort. Some of the reductions were made by outplacing the managers who claimed that they could not find the resources for change.

ASSUMPTION 2.15
ALL CHANGE PROJECTS MUST HAVE NEARLY FULL-TIME SUPPORT FROM THE EXECUTIVES OF THE BUSINESS.

When a project fails, many excuses are given. One of the most frequent is that the project lacked sufficient executive-level attention. The fact that this assumption is believed by many executives is the reason such excuses carry any weight. Actually, the assumption is almost always invalid, and the excuses that rely upon it are usually just plain balderdash.

For really detailed, step-by-step workflow change projects, it has been our experience that the working-level participants should indeed be taken out of their daily jobs and put to work on the project full time. It is also a good idea to recruit one or two first-level managers on the same basis. However, the levels above should participate in reciprocal proportion to their levels:

Working level—100 percent

1st-level mangers—one or two at 100 percent, several others in and out of the team as required

2nd-level—one, two, or three meetings per week

3rd-level (usually the project sponsor)—one meeting per week

Levels above—one presentation at the end of the project

The level of participation does not change simply because the project has high visibility or is deemed extraordinarily important. Participation in a project should be determined by the help that each person can offer, not by how curious senior management is about the details of the project. These recommended levels of involvement assume a high degree of delegation, commonly known as empowerment, which is essential to the success of any project. The lack of empowerment can cause a project to fail, but the failure of senior management to spend all or most of its time drawing pictures of workflow processes is never the reason for a botched effort.

ASSUMPTION 2.16
THE CHANGE PROJECT MUST BE BOTTOM-UP TO OBTAIN THE COMMITMENT OF THE STAFF. SIMILARLY, IT MUST BE TOP-DOWN FOR IT TO BE SUPPORTED BY MANAGEMENT.

There are two common approaches for a company to take when it starts making changes. The traditional approach is to begin with the top level of management, assuring the project of approval, attention, and direction, and then to work down toward the lowest level at which the work is done. This method has been used for hundreds of years, beginning with the military organizations of antiquity. It continues today with the work of contemporary management practices and industrial engineering. Senior managers have never complained about it. The other common approach is the bottom-up method, favored by organization development methodology and by the modern quest for quality that is based upon the work of W. Edwards Deming.

Each of these approaches has merit. The top-down approach provides executive vision and strategy, both developed from a company-wide point of view and based upon many years of management experience. The bottom-up approach has the advantage of building staff commitment, and can also address a level of detail that senior management generally knows little about. It is not the approaches themselves that are impediments, but the unquestioned assumption that either one or the other is absolutely valid. There are reasons for starting projects at either end of the management spectrum in any business, but in each case the advantages of the opposite approach must be also be obtained. For example, top-down projects can seek employee commitment by offering special incentives, and bottom-up projects can be made to address strategic issues by employing cross-project communications.

There is also a third, completely different change project starting point, one used by the authors with some success. It is called "middle-out." A middle-out approach starts with middle management and works both up and down. It has the advantage of a wider point of view than bottom-up, but it is close enough to the working level to address the details that are the lifeblood of process management improvement.

ASSUMPTION 2.17
THE BIGGEST PROBLEM IS FIGURING OUT WHAT TO CHANGE. DECIDING HOW TO CHANGE IT WILL THEN BE EASY.

This assumption has been an obstacle to progress in business for a long time. It is the result of the dominant approach to change in large businesses, an approach that is usually comprised of the following steps:

1. Management decides that there is a problem that must be addressed.

2. A study is conducted by outside consultants and/or company managers and staff.

3. The results of the study are presented formally.

4. Management decides which, if any, of the study's recommendations are to be implemented.

5. One manager is made responsible for the implementation, usually someone who has taken some part in the study.

6. The manager prepares and presents a plan and a budget for the implementation.

7. The implementation plan is either accepted or rejected by management, and then may either begin, or else (of course) wait.

8. The implementation project is executed, with reporting to the senior managers who approved it.

The massive problems inherent in this approach have been ignored for many years. There are distinct barriers between some of the steps that break the continuity of the approach, and there is far too much concentration on the study. The analysts are motivated to come up with dramatic results, whether they can be implemented in the real world or not. Only recently has the assumption that this is the only way to conduct change been challenged successfully. Modern change methodologies provide better approaches, but this assumption is still quite common in all forms of business, and the old pattern of change remains.

A Midwestern petrochemical company wanted to make itself more efficient. They hired a prestigious consulting firm to reengineer an important business process. The first step was a study to design a process. The study took a year and cost over ten million dollars. When the report was issued, it was satisfyingly long: several volumes. However, upon examination, it was discovered that the recommendations could not possibly be implemented. The company initiated a lawsuit to recover not only what it had paid, but its lost opportunities. The matter was settled out of court for only the amount it had paid to the consulting company.

ASSUMPTION 2.18
CHANGE SHOULD START WITH A BLANK SHEET OF PAPER.

The idea that change should start with a blank sheet of paper has been around much longer than Michael Hammer's famous advice: "Don't automate, obliterate!" as he entitled his *Harvard Business Review* article. He was interested in making an audacious public statement, and he succeeded. This assumption can also be based on the opinion, *lucus a non lucendo,* that Japanese business succeeded to the degree that it did because Japan was bombed and therefore was forced to build brand-new factories. That factor was not the basis of Japanese success.

Even before the late 1970s, when Japan became a top-level industrial force, many consultants and systems analysts started with blank paper when designing organizations, computer systems, and business approaches to replace existing ones. The rationale was that they did not want to be unduly influenced by the practices of the past, which is certainly laudable. But throwing out everything that exists today is absurd.

Is nothing worth saving in your company? Is nothing at all being done right? Does the company have no competitive advantage whatsoever? If so, then there is indeed nothing desirable from the past to carry forward. However, even in cases where everything is wrong, it is still necessary to study the present situation, for the following reasons:

1. *It is necessary to look at the present to determine all of the requirements for the future.* Some details are easily overlooked if the change project elects the traditional approach: to go directly into the new design, determining requirements out of whole cloth or just by interviewing the staff who are doing the current work. In the past there may be many mistakes, but there is also the knowledge that only comes from learning the business the hard way.

2. *To move from the current operation to the new one, it is necessary to know what the current operation is doing.* The only alternatives are to discontinue the current operation while implementing the new one, which results in a hiatus of products and services (and cash flow), or to build the new alongside the old, which requires duplication of resources and expense.

These reasons are enough to start with the current operation rather than a blank sheet. There are others, such as the inability to design a feasible new operation without a starting point, the inability to use any existing technology support for any operation designed from scratch, and the psychological trauma for the staff, among many others. Here is a good example of a very well-run change project, a project that made only one mistake: starting with a blank sheet.

One of the pioneers of business process reengineering, an aerospace company in which leadership was almost a habit, reengineered its most important business process. Its objective was to cut the cost of its products by 40 percent so as to win competitive procurement contracts. Their entire process was redesigned and restructured to manufacture products of the same or better quality at much lower cost in much less time. The effort was a success.

Ten years later, this company ran into serious cost overrun problems. They were called before a U.S. Congressional committee to explain themselves. The problem was that during the reengineering process, they had deleted key audits from the work. That nearly cost them their whole business and they have been forced to sell themselves to a larger firm. Key work steps had been lost because they had started with a blank sheet and some essential tasks had fallen through the cracks, so to speak. It would have been easy enough to avoid this problem by starting instead with complete knowledge of their current processes.

ASSUMPTION 2.19
MANAGEMENT DOES NOT WANT TO HEAR ANY BAD NEWS.

The assumption is commonly made that management, particularly senior management, does not want to hear any bad news. It is also thought that management does not want to hear any opinions that differ from theirs. These assumptions are invalid in the vast majority of cases. Most managers want to know bad news as soon as possible, and will consider any opinion that might help improve any phase of the work for which they are responsible.

There are certainly some good reasons for assuming management might not want to hear bad news. No one likes hearing about failures, problems, and losses, so the first reaction of any manager may not be to praise the bearer of such information. It is also true that some managers discourage honesty and initiative. Some remarkably inferior supervisors even do it knowingly. However, most forget that this assumption is a natural one and must be actively challenged in the normal course of managing. If it is not, it will almost always be assumed that any negative communication is unwanted.

A very large international financial institution had a large travel budget, and was supported for many years by a single travel agency whose contract had never been competed against. The decision was made at a senior level to invite competition for the travel services contract, and the travel services manager was given the responsibility for the procurement. When the senior vice president gave the travel services manager this job, he discussed senior management's motivation. During the discussion, the concept of using two competing travel agencies was brought up, and the travel services manager was told that senior management wanted this sort of arrangement.

The competition was run fairly, in accordance with corporate policy. However, the procurement panel was made aware of senior management's purported desire for two winners, and no alternative was given serious consideration, despite the misgivings of the panel. Two contracts were awarded.

Several years later, the two-agency concept had clearly failed. The agencies fought with each other and the benefits of competition were far outweighed by the inconveniences and inconsistencies between the two vendors. There was also some loss of rebates when compared with using a single travel services vendor. All of this had been anticipated by the procurement panel, but ignored due to their misperception of management's wishes. Senior managers disavowed having put any pressure on the procurement panel, saying that the panel had full authority to decide whether one or two agencies were to be used, and that senior management only wanted the two-agency approach to be fully considered. This decision, a poor decision as it turned out, was based on the assumption that management did not want to have an opinion differing from their own come out of the procurement panel's deliberations. It is impossible to determine how strong senior management's aversion to the panel's real views would have been, but there was no real attempt to confront the issues during the procurement process.

ASSUMPTION 2.20
SWEAT THE DETAILS, AND THE REST WILL TAKE CARE OF ITSELF.

The first part of this assumption is good advice. The details are important, and someone must pay close attention to them. However, the old saying about being penny-wise and pound-foolish has truth to it as well. Taking care of the details is not all there is to do in a business. It is certainly a poor approach to change. Indeed, the details can easily hide the larger issues. Tactics concern details, but strategy does not.

One way to look at organizational responsibilities is that the higher in the organization a manager sits, the longer into the future his or her attention ought to be focused. Senior executives should be concentrating on the distant future, which today may be as close as the next quarter, but their planning will be strategic, and their level of detail broad. While there is a place for the details, it is not in planning change, determining strategy, or looking at how improvement can take place. It is only in the most detailed part of the implementation that one must "sweat the details." Here is a good example, showing that this assumption can have widespread and significant impact even when it is held by only one executive.

Some time ago, a large Midwestern company placed much of its change management under a senior executive who prided himself on his "sweating the details" philosophy. This assignment effectively stalled the company's improvement schedule by over a year.

To promote his philosophy throughout his organization, the senior executive gathered all his vice presidents together for a two- to three-hour meeting weekly. Each was asked to discuss in detail the progress to date, and what was expected to happen during the next week. This was in addition to frequent detailed one-on-one meetings that the executive held daily with each one of the people reporting directly to him. Because he believed in direct control, he felt that he must approve all actions, no matter how minute, before any initiative was undertaken. Progress was slowed by these meetings and his approval process, but it seemed to give him the control he wanted. However, his subordinates did not react as well as he wanted. The behavior exhibited by these vice presidents included:

- lack of initiative,
- fear of failure,

- lack of commitment, and
- frustration.

The results of the apparent gain of control for the senior executive were also negative for the business. His micromanagement hurt the company in the following ways:

- delayed projects,
- excessive time in meetings, and
- lack of creativity.

This company essentially learned that empowering employees to perform independently is critical to success. This was especially true after units had been downsized. The remaining staff were only able to function when they were allowed to move quickly, learn from the experience, and move forward again. This senior executive learned that a good coach is not the one who is out on the floor playing the game. Good coaches do not win games, they help their teams win.

For each possible business strategy, there are many different sets of details. One of middle management's most important responsibilities is assuring the relevance of every detail to the company's strategy. It is very easy to forget about strategy when focusing on details, but it can be a very bad practice. Just don't do it.

CHALLENGING GENERAL BUSINESS ASSUMPTIONS

General assumptions, like anything else that affects an entire business, are the direct responsibility of senior management. The best possible attack on any company's invalid assumptions will come from the highest office in the company. It is as much a matter of leadership as of analysis and problem solving.

Challenging assumptions is also a change in culture for most companies. Too many businesses run on a form of inertia. When a company runs on inertia, senior management has only the illusion of control over the business operation. When changes are desired, they just seem to have no effect. Complete reorganizations have failed because of the stubbornness of corporate culture and the inertia it engenders. Senior managers who are aware of this problem ask how culture can be changed; challenging assumptions is certainly one of the best ways to do this.

However, some of the problems described in this chapter are best solved by simple good management on the part of the CEO and the senior management team. It is their responsibility to correct the company's communication problems. It is also the job of every company's most senior management to take fear out of the business. The CEO alone is responsible for the development of genuine teamwork, and the methods are simply those of good management.

Change is a different matter. A large part of controlling any company is the ability to understand the true nature of change. Realistically, a company that controls change can use it as a competitive advantage. This ability is important in taking advantage of opportunity and responding to competitive, market, and financial pressures.

To control change, most businesses need a new approach. Constant change is now a necessity. Change must no longer be feared, but accepted as the opportunity that it can truly become. However, very lengthy change processes can no longer be tolerated, because they pose an unreasonable risk. Speed is the single most important factor in change today.

Consistency is also important in managing change, since the increased rate of change will make individualized approaches completely untenable. Business's increased rate of change makes the ability to measure the results of change increasingly important as well. These new requirements make the use of innovative, effective change methodologies a critical success factor for all businesses.

CHANGE METHODOLOGIES

The first step in improving change management is to either draft or adopt a formal change management methodology. This simple step will provide two important improvements: (1) changes can be made consistently over time and throughout the company, and (2) each change will itself be thorough, having a complete checklist of success factors. Examples of complete change management methodologies are Xerox's *SMI*, the European Consulting Group's *Methodica*, and MTB's own *Dynamic Business Process Re-engineering*. They all have the same basic characteristics:

1. They all analyze the current state first.
2. They all require the specification of how the results of the change will be measured.
3. They all specify steps for a change project, and formal reviews for each step.
4. They are all supported by techniques for each phase of work.

These methodologies also provide various levels of advice concerning the roles of management and facilitators. They all show how to organize for effective group work, and each contains advice related to analytical methods for the full range of problems that business can address through change projects. They can all be applied to a new overall approach to making change work better, called "evolutive management."

EVOLUTIVE MANAGEMENT

There is a better way to manage change—one that overcomes the obstacles of invalid assumptions and the attitudes behind them.

Evolutive management is an approach to managing a company through the use of continual improvement in the form of fast, controlled changes. These changes can:

- increase the quality of products and services,
- increase the company's internal flexibility and ability to respond to market fluctuations and new business opportunities (change readiness), and
- make operational improvements of all sorts.

Evolutive management allows business to use change to create a competitive advantage. Change becomes an ally, instead of an enemy, to both the corporation and its employees. Evolutive management differs from current practices by associating and combining all improvement and strategic implementation (tactics and projects) into a continual flow of change. Change is not viewed as specific isolated projects, nor is it obtained through long-drawn-out projects. Evolutive management rather builds on the fact that all parts of a company are interdependent, and, to effect real improvement, all of the affected parts of the operation must change together. Change is thus made to both process and organization structure at the same time. Following evolutive management, change methods are built into the routine procedures of a company. Thus comprehensive understanding of change methods, process improvement, the company's business operation, and its organizational structure are all required, and are used by all managers continually.

Most business people still consider change a disruptive factor, one that should be avoided unless there is no alternative. In the past change has often been disruptive, and it is very frightening to all employees who are working in rigid, old-fashioned corporate cultures. In these cultures, change is seldom recognized for what it really is and it is almost never effectively controlled. Also, the problems associated with change have often been exacerbated by outside consultants. One response to the problems of change from many of the big consulting companies was the use of cumbersome and exacting methodologies. These methodologies (like most approaches from consultants) try to cover almost everything conceivable, in the belief that the solutions must lie somewhere in the detail. The techniques used by these firms have resulted in unacceptably high failure rates and ever-tightening rigidity. Neither can be accepted.

Change can be viewed as a flow of interwoven actions. Some are lengthy, involving many of the company's workforce, while others are brief and involve only a few. However, the complexity and scope of each action are not necessarily in direct proportion to its importance. It is the impact that determines its importance, and the impact of any change activity affects all aspects of the company's work to some degree. Evolutive management recognizes this key attribute of change, and specifies that all impacts, including indirect ones, be identified so that they may be anticipated.

The indirect impacts of change are identified from several points of view. The first is the impact of any change upon the way the work is done. If the company knows what its business processes are, the impacts are identified for each. The second point of view is the organization structure; the impacts upon each organizational unit and major impacts on individual employees are identified. The third viewpoint is measurement. What business measurement systems will be affected, which specific measurements must be changed, and how can historical data be gathered or estimated for comparison to new measurements? Finally, evolutive management looks at information technology and specifies modifications to the company's technology architecture, communications, data architecture, and software systems.

After identifying the full impact of proposed changes, the costs and benefits of these changes can be determined much more accurately than in the past. Because more is known in advance, better estimates can be given. Once the impact is known and the potential costs and benefits are defined, management can make much more informed decisions. The change is performed based on planned objectives and consistent, but flexible, methods that are based on the incremental creation and deployment of the change. This incremental approach cuts risk, speeds up the process of change, and focuses on benefits. It also allows the change to be built in a way that front-ends all high-benefit actions to provide a much more satisfying return on investment curve.

Evolutive management makes use of brief, high-impact projects to provide incremental benefits. But it is more closely managed and quantified than just setting the workforce upon a program of continuing improvement, as Deming suggested. Improving in small increments poses much less risk and provides quicker returns than the traditional company-shattering major project approach to managing change. Evolutive management also brings the company's change management into close alignment with daily operations management, so that:

a. the company always knows where it is; change is not managed month-to-month or quarter-to-quarter, but day-to-day;

b. changes are determined by operations line managers, not by staff or consultants.

Evolution affects everyone in the company. Everything in the company is interrelated, every action has a reaction. Sooner or later the ripple of any action will affect others. In significant changes, each employee will be either an active or a passive part of the modification. Business improvement must be viewed as a pervasive and invasive entity.

The objective of evolutive management is speed tempered only by accuracy. Perfection is not its objective: no single change project is meant either to achieve an ultimate goal nor to achieve a partial goal perfectly. Each change is to be completed quickly and to achieve results that are just adequate to solve the problem or exploit the opportunity at hand.

The design of a proposed change is reviewed for feasibility, cost, impact, and the probability that it will provide the needed support. This review is not exhaustive, and consensus is not required. After they are planned and approved, changes are made in controlled increments. As each increment goes into production, it is reviewed and any problems discovered are corrected on the fly. Evolutive management is change management on the run. It is a process of continual tuning, constantly improving the business in small steps.

This approach is directly opposite to that recommended by the large public accounting firms. It is indeed based on a wholly different concept. It seems impulsive and incautious. It avoids large projects and the illusion of control that is usually associated with large projects. But the rate of change in business today requires a new approach. The old one just doesn't work any longer, if it ever really did.

While some may disagree with the emphasis on speed, few can disagree with the need to limit risk, disruption, and failure. Evolutive management does all these things. Where applied, this approach has never failed.

IMPLEMENTING AN EVOLUTIVE MANAGEMENT APPROACH

While this topic deserves a whole book to itself, there are several basic steps that can be described here. Each will provide an immediate improvement. However, there is some political risk inherent in moving to evolutive management. It will shake up the *status quo*.

The first step in evolutive management is to examine and chronicle how the business actually operates, how the work is done, how every activity relates to every other activity. This is no small job, but it is necessary. A complete picture of the business will provide the ability to anticipate the impact of change. It is best to use a computer program for this step; process is too complex to be jotted down on the back of an envelope.

Next, stop any long-term projects and refocus them. Begin by dividing them into manageable increments and then reevaluating each of these increments. Does each one still make good business sense? Do they all move the company closer to its strategic goals? For the newly refocused projects that are judged important to the company, a new flexible but consistent approach or methodology should be adopted. This new methodology will assure quality and a reasonable level of standardization among all change projects, and make them easier to manage and review. All unnecessary controls and non-value-added steps in the company's change methods should be eliminated, of course.

The redesigned projects can then be restarted. In addition to managing these projects using the new change management methodology, attention should be given to engaging the affected staff and managers in the changes that are being made. They should feel that the changes belong to them and that they are responsible to the company for specific aspects of each change. Management should provide perspective, fully adequate resources, and rapid review of the recommendations of each project.

Finally, since technology is often the most expensive and time-consuming area to change in a large business, attention should be given to it. The technology environment should be evaluated with change-readiness in mind. It must be stable but flexible. Technology supports every aspect of business today, so excuses cannot be accepted for technology that is not fulfilling its planned objectives. In reviewing technology, a list of the actions needed to provide stability and flexibility should be developed. The actual improvement of the information services operation ought to be approached as an evolutionary process, just as the rest of the business processes are.

WHO DOES EVOLUTIVE MANAGEMENT?

One of the important aspects of evolutive management is that daily operations and change management are combined. Every manager is as accountable for improving the operation as for running it. Indeed, every employee has a role in moving the company toward a better posture as they do their daily work. This approach is not new; it was a key element of Deming's advice twenty years ago. The rest of an evolutive manager's job is much the same as what good managers are expected to practice today:

- Strip out fear and blame;
- Institute experimentation and energize the staff;
- Establish, maintain, and even test good communications; invite immediate reporting of problems and even criticism;
- Insist upon teamwork and cooperation among direct reports; discourage selfish behavior; as for allowing harmful assumptions to make your decisions for you: just don't do it.

CUSTOMER RELATIONSHIP ASSUMPTIONS

ARE YOUR CUSTOMER RELATIONSHIPS AS GOOD AS YOU THINK THEY ARE?

If you build a better mousetrap, you must still open your doors. Every business person knows the value of customer service, just as they are all aware of the importance of marketing. Simply building a good product has never been enough, and there is no assumption to the contrary. Customer service is also not a back-burner issue. Ever since the 1980s, when Tom Peters began the refocusing of business attention onto the customer, companies have wrestled with the dilemma of improving the interactions between their employees and their customers. Surprisingly, little visible improvement is apparent. The customers certainly don't see it. Studies and consulting experiences over the past five years indicate that while most companies are attempting to refocus on the customer, few have succeeded.

The many excellent Peters books and lectures showcase companies that actually have succeeded. He found much of the excellence that he searched for in new ways to satisfy customers. Recently, consultants have come across an increasing number of companies that are very much like Tom Peters' case studies. Here is one good example.

The Kane County Cougars, a minor league baseball team in northern Illinois, has made itself a profitable venture by the same customer-oriented methods as Peters described, adding their own flourishes to increase the appeal of the games to the whole family. The Cougars have specific children's activities, such as young audience contests and clowns. The customer service details are thoroughly covered. Example: a customer who was leaving long before the middle of the game was stopped by an usher and asked why. Hearing that the customer could not find a good spot on the lawn (the lawn is the cheapest area, of course), the usher seated the customer in an unused season-ticket box (the most expensive seats) at no charge. The staff are empowered to do whatever they can to satisfy every customer. Their games are always sold out.

So why doesn't every business behave that way? Some have actually made conscious decisions to discourage certain behaviors in customers by ignoring them or treating them rudely. Some others have trimmed customer service costs knowing and accepting the results, a shortsighted practice in almost every case. There are whole industries that fail to meet the lowest standards in customer relations, each business protected by the failings of the others. Airlines, taxicab operators, and cable television companies are infamously unresponsive to their clientele. These companies are simply inviting competition, and most of them know it. But many other companies believe that they are trying to improve customer relations and are just not aware that they are not actually doing so.

So much attention has been paid to the area of customer relations that many effective customer relationship approaches are well known. Customer orientation, empowerment of staff in contact with customers, shortening the chain of work and decision activities performed in response to customer requirements, and special training in behavior toward customers are almost universally recognized as beneficial. However, there has been little dissemination of the methods by which these approaches can be implemented. Many of the success stories (like the Kane County Cougars) are found to be relatively small companies, in which the CEO can make improvements personally. Large companies present a real challenge. A mere edict from the managing committee will not result in much enhancement of behavior toward customers. Almost no one realizes that they are not handling customers as well as they can, in the circumstances imposed by the business. Some companies have gone so far as to establish a very high-level position to improve their customer relations, with only mixed success.

THE INSIGHT THAT FAILED

Even in the face of considerable executive commitment, quantum improvements in customer relations have been elusive. Several factors contribute to this problem, not the least of which is that many attempts to improve customer service have been conducted side by side with (or immediately following) downsizing (or right-sizing, as it sometimes euphemistically labeled). It is very difficult to bludgeon the workforce and, simultaneously, expect them to be more positive in their customer relations. This is one of the many reasons for unpredicted losses of business after mass outplacements. The order of these two types of company improvements might be effectively reversed: improving customer relations first and cutting staff afterward (possibly cutting some of those who do not respond to customer relations initiatives). Unfortunately, this approach is made unattractive by the securities markets' reactions. Strangely, the common stock of companies that downsize almost always shows an increase, while investors seldom notice improvements in customer relations. Since the primary responsibility of profit-making companies is to increase stockholder equity, there is generally less short-term motivation to improve customer satisfaction than there is to reduce costs. In the long term, however, few business people question the need to improve customer relations. Another reason that customer relations is not a short-term performance booster is that most CR improvements can't be done very quickly. They require analysis, design, training, and often experimentation.

Because improving customer relations involves so much time and so many people, it will probably benefit any company to challenge its assumptions in this area before setting out to make improvements.

ASSUMPTION 3.1
SOMEONE IN THE COMPANY KNOWS THE CUSTOMERS AND WHAT IS IMPORTANT TO THEM.

This assumption arises from the diversity in large corporations. Each specialized part makes assumptions about the others, individually or collectively. It is not uncommon for the entire company to relegate any and all knowledge about customers to the marketing and sales staff. However, the marketing and sales groups may feel that they know customer profiles well, but that the operations staff who are in contact with customers know them personally and understand their problems better. These views may or may not be wholly correct, but the existence of a combination of all this customer knowledge almost never happens. The company as a whole is unaware of this critical information deficit.

Here is an example of a company that did not have key information about how it was treating its customers, and how the customers were reacting.

A large publishing company carried this assumption to an extreme that almost resulted in its complete ruin. The company sold reference material that was time sensitive. Updates were sent out weekly to report changes in the information that they published. The marketing and sales activities had based their efforts on service packages that contained various combinations of subscriptions. These packages began with piece-by-piece material. This was the service that all their large subscription clients were receiving. Their sales objective was to increase the amount of material to which each large customer subscribed, which they called "raising the customer to a higher level."

When they succeeded in selling a higher level product package, the sales force issued instructions to begin mailing the increased material level and also to stop the current, lower level of material. The sales group received no feedback from their customers, nor from the publisher's internal operations staff, to verify the actual execution of these instructions. In practice, the stop order for the current level of printed material was executed very efficiently, and took effect within a month, often less. But the order for the increased level of material took up to 90 days. This left the customer without any material at all for up to two months. Many customers complained, and the complaints were forwarded to one of the many order departments in the company, but no one in the company had a full picture of the problem. No one knew the customers' viewpoint of the company's services, although it was widely assumed that someone did.

The company saw its best customers, customers who had recently placed orders, going to the competition. Neither senior management nor the sales group knew why. A consulting company was engaged to improve the order process. The consultants interviewed staff throughout the company. The interviews resulted, many times, in the significant statement: "Of course someone knows this ... someone must know." But until the situation was examined by an outside agency, no one did know, and the results were very costly.

The company's competition had learned to follow sales calls and to sell to the company's best customers when their services had been shut off. Obviously, the ultimate solution to this problem was to fulfill orders for increased service faster, but the short-term solution was clearly just not cutting off the current service.

ASSUMPTION 3.2
THE CUSTOMER IS A FACELESS STRANGER, WHOSE BEHAVIOR CAN ONLY BE GUESSED AT.

Customers are real people. They communicate their values, opinions, and requirements whenever they feel enough compulsion to do so. But many businesses do not readily accept and absorb this vital data. It passes right under the noses of salespersons, order processing clerks, customer service representatives, and even accounting staff, but except in rare cases it is not passed on to others who might be able to use it. Most companies simply do not believe there is anything to be gained in studying customer behavior outside of the marketing function.

This is another assumption that applies most often to large companies. Small companies are much more likely to have personal relationships with customers throughout their structures. In large companies, only the sales staff are likely to know the company's clients, and then only the ones with whom they deal directly. Customer service staff have infrequent contacts (hopefully), so they only become familiar with customers who have recurring problems. Even customers with many problems are often not serviced by the same personnel, since there are very few companies that even try to find out if a customer has had prior contact with customer service and reassign the same representative.

These contact patterns tend to make profiling individual customers difficult, to be sure. It is not necessarily profitable to record and use each contact's individualities, but that does not mean that none exist, and that is often the assumption.

This assumption results in a number of problems. First, the customer contact functions (sales, ordering, customer service, etc.) will try to find one contact method and instrument (such as an order form) that will fit every customer, when using several types may be a much better approach (for the customer). For example, some companies vary their ordering practices by geographical region. Secondly, the company may make sweeping changes to its practices as a result of a few exceptions, instead of developing efficient ways to handle exceptions. A fundamental reason for complex, undocumented workflow is that changes of this sort occur over long periods. Knowing the customers well results in their exceptional behavior being treated as exceptions by the business. If, however, the assumption is made that the customer can't be known, the workflows will slowly evolve into doing exceptional work for all customers all the time. But workflows need not become so complex. Get to know the customers, and just don't assume that every customer requires exceptional practices.

ASSUMPTION 3.3
EMPLOYEES UNDERSTAND THE VALUE OF CUSTOMERS, SO OF COURSE THEY WILL BE NICE TO THEM.

One of the most basic assumptions related to customer relations is that the need for them is obvious to every employee in the business. Indeed, this would seem to be a valid assumption. Why would anyone think otherwise? How could any incident of trouble with a customer not be an exception, a case of an employee who is normally polite and cooperative being driven to an unusual remark by a particularly rude customer in especially frustrating circumstances?

Unfortunately, there are many employees who know quite well that their company needs customers to stay in business, but who do not consider that the individual customer with whom they are dealing is worth the effort of being either polite or cooperative. They often assume that there are some customers who just cannot be satisfied, no matter what is done. Other employees have no real interest in any customer's satisfaction. There may be some truth to the first assumption, but if so it is only true in a very small percentage of cases. There is no excuse whatever for the second.

The most common reason for being defensive, curt, or unresponsive to customers is being unconscious of this behavior. It grows over time, possibly in response to the pressures of work, and very often out of the perceived need to enforce company policies at the expense of the customers. It is a very natural problem, and it will arise in the absence of positive preventive measures. These must include a way to sample customer contacts and to feed back the results to both the representative and management. The relationship between the company and the staff who are responsible for customer contacts is also a factor. If there are bad feelings toward the company, it is likely that the representative will pass bad feelings on to the customer.

Most retail businesses pay some attention to customer relations, and do not automatically assume their customers are getting the right treatment. However, even these companies feel that if they have emphasized the importance of customers, the staff can be relied upon to do the right thing. This is true only to the point that they have been taught the right things to do for all customer response situations. And even then, some lessons may not have been learned.

Another factor associated with this assumption is empowerment. It is often assumed that if management has taken special steps to empower the customer service representative, the representative will be able to act independently. This ability is frequently limited by the representative's actual authority and knowledge. It is also limited by representatives' feeling uncertain of the limits of their authority, and fearing reprisal if they are too generous.

This assumption is too common, and invalid much more often than supposed. It need not be. It is very easy to challenge, and it should be challenged frequently.

ASSUMPTION 3.4
CUSTOMERS WILL TOLERATE ALMOST ANYTHING.

There are a few businesses which, in limited circumstances, maintain a deliberately unpleasant customer interface. They are usually intended to discourage customers from forcing the expenditure of effort that is perceived as unrewarding to the enterprise. These deterrents are almost always set up either in areas where the customers are not valued, or where the assumption is made that the customers will tolerate any treatment. This assumption also sometimes finds its way into customer service areas that are not intended to discourage customers, where it is completely inexplicable.

For example, several airlines are supplying really low-quality customer service on the telephone sales lines that are their most profitable market. No customer need tolerate any delay when ordering a ticket from an airline. They always have recourse to other carriers and to travel agencies that the airlines must pay out of their own pockets. In understaffing and underequipping their own sales outlets, these airlines are making a serious mistake. The assumption behind this mistake is that their customers will tolerate the delays for a time, and so they staff seasonally and only slowly take on more staff for the heavy seasons after the demand assures them of keeping the new staff busy. The customer contacts made in these sales channels are apparently not seen as opportunities to build customer loyalty and to win customers away from travel agencies (except in the minor area of referrals to car rental companies). If they challenged the assumption that customers will put up with delays, they might experience a considerable increase in revenue.

Delays are not the only thing that customers are supposed to tolerate. Companies will try to sidestep promises (see Assumption 3.6), staff customer contact points with underqualified personnel, switch goods that have been ordered, change specifications and prices without notice, and utterly fail to make up for obvious mistakes in any manner. Some customers will tolerate some of these things some of the time. No one will tolerate them for very long. This is a very damaging assumption, the mark of a company that is very badly managed or is milking its customer base with no thought for future growth.

ASSUMPTION 3.5
REMOVING THE CUSTOMER FROM HUMAN CONTACT IS GOOD.

A common assumption when process changes are being made is that providing human contact for customers at various points in the process is expensive and unreliable, and should therefore be minimized. Any contact that can be made by mechanical means is assumed to be more cost efficient and in most cases more effective. Communication services (telephones) are a good example of this assumption, and indeed may have been the leaders in mechanizing customer contact.

This assumption can be true in limited circumstances, but it can only be true if the mechanical or computer contact is satisfactory for both the customer and the company. For example, the contact should be designed to provide feedback that would be obtained from a person-to-person contact. Also, since corporate customer service staff must be managed, personal contacts should be capable of referring any situation to a manager or supervisor. Thus a computerized contact must have some sort of escalation capability deliberately designed into it, usually escalation out of the mechanical response system and to a staff member. Another design factor is the number of steps that a customer must take to get the desired result from the automated system. There are several potential levels of frustration that must be carefully assessed.

The most basic question regarding automated customer service is whether to use it or not. The assumption that any form of automated contact is superior to a human one is incorrect. Automated responses may or may not be beneficial, depending upon how much judgment is required in the contact—judgment on both sides, customer and company. It is also necessary to test the capabilities of the automated system, to avoid the assumption that if automation is present, it will always do its job. It is a common practice to reduce secretarial services in favor of word processors, electronic mail, and voice mail. But most voice mail facilities have a limited capacity, and fill up whenever the recipient is away for more than a few days. This can make some of the company's staff completely inaccessible from outside the company for protracted periods of time. Just don't do it.

ASSUMPTION 3.6
IT IS NOT NECESSARY TO LIVE UP TO THE PROMISES THE BUSINESS MAKES.

In some industries more than in others, the marketing of products and services is quite separate from the business operation. The result is that marketing makes promises that operations does not feel obligated to keep. This is a common problem in banking, for example. Marketing in the banking industry has generally been limited to advertising, and has had very little to do with activities such as product development that actually influence the way services are delivered. As banking competition has increased, the relationship between marketing and operations has improved to the point that it is now more common for marketing to have a role in interest rate setting and the locations and services offered by branches, but there are still promises being made that operations does not fulfill. Banking is not alone in this practice, especially where guarantees are made.

Most product guarantees are limited by the well-known mechanism of fine print restrictions. In some cases, the restrictions are merely inherent in the wording of the guarantee, or in assumptions that might be made by customers. An example is the supposedly complete camera insurance sold by a large eastern chain of camera stores. Covered products are protected against any hazard, even abuse by the owner. This would seem to be adequate protection, but an incident observed recently shows that even ironclad guarantees can be inadequate.

A customer brought a camera that had been run over by her own automobile into one of a large camera chain's stores. It was smashed almost beyond recognition, and the guarantee that she bought with the camera said that it would be repaired, or replaced if it could not be repaired. It was clearly not capable of being repaired, but the assistant manager of the store declared that he could not replace it under the warranty. By the rules of the store, the camera had to be sent to the chain's central repair facility to be declared irreparable. That would take two weeks, during which time the customer would be without a camera and hopping mad. The assistant manager was not empowered to do anything to alleviate the problem.

Since there was no doubt of the final outcome, why did the camera store throw away that customer? They had made the assumption that the letter of their contract was sufficient—there was no need to satisfy a perceived promise. A very false assumption and a false economy on the part of the camera chain.

ASSUMPTION 3.7
THE CUSTOMER WILL FIND THE RIGHT PEOPLE IN THE COMPANY TO TALK TO.

The assumption that customers will find the right place in the company to transact whatever business they have in mind persists despite much evidence to the contrary and even, amazingly, in the face of new technologies that make proper contact much easier. Any company can afford an automated call routing system that has a simple push-button menu.

Companies that seem to be deliberately denying effective points of contact are often just the victims of this assumption. Even internal company staff have trouble locating the right people in large companies. Only a very small number of companies, mostly in service industries, have taken the trouble to produce a set of comprehensive functional telephone listings, publish them for internal use, and given them to their telephone operators so that their clientele can benefit from them as well.

One advance in handling customers on the telephone is progressing well: instances of customers being asked to call another number are decreasing. The policy of having the company call back is now the rule rather than the exception in such service-intensive businesses as computer technology. Indeed, this policy is the only way to deal with the very heavy customer service requirements generated by new technologies without spending prohibitively large amounts on the customer service function. It is especially important to be effective in locating the right person and not requiring long waiting times, when, to save costs, the company requires the caller to pay long-distance tolls.

So the technology and the techniques exist to locate the right person with just one call in any business. But full implementation is far from universal. Because most businesses do not routinely test the telephone or mail approaches to their infrastructures, they assume that they are working well when often they are not. This is another area in which there is little excuse for failure.

ASSUMPTION 3.8
CUSTOMERS WILL MAKE DECISIONS THAT ARE IN THEIR OWN BEST INTERESTS.

Most companies make the assumption that their customers will act in their own best interests, and this assumption seems obviously correct. However, there are two problems with this assumption. First, it is assumed that customers will recognize where their best interests lie; but they often do not. Second, it is assumed that if customers can discern their best interests they will always act upon them; but they sometimes will not.

In many cases it is very difficult for customers to know exactly what will produce the best results for them, especially in making decisions about the procurement of services. Customers are influenced by many emotional factors and are often overinfluenced by pricing for services, when they cannot see or touch differences in quality and when they are persuaded by misleading promises.

The only way to gauge customer reactions is by careful observation of actual customer behavior. Market studies are often helpful, but they are not foolproof. The notorious revision of the formula for Coca-Cola was market-tested in many blind taste tests, but the product failed when it actually came to market. There is an amusing example of an entrepreneur challenging this assumption almost 500 years ago.

Customer capriciousness is revealed in the histories of the tomato and the potato when each was introduced into Europe. The tomato, called the "love apple," was introduced with many promises. In fact it was overenthusiastically marketed. The results for the first few decades were very disappointing. The tomato was rumored to be poisonous and was shunned. Walter Raleigh learned from the lesson of the tomato and tried a different ploy with potatoes. He was introduced to potatoes by Native Americans. He brought potatoes back to England, but did not try to grow and sell them there. Instead, Raleigh put his potatoes in a walled garden on his estate in Ireland, and forbade anyone to take so much as a leaf from the plants. The gate to the garden was locked. He even posted armed guards. The success of the potato in Ireland was the result. Raleigh was a shrewd judge of behavior. He did not assume his potential customers would act in their best interest.

ASSUMPTION 3.9
THE CUSTOMER WILL ACCEPT VALUE AND QUALITY AS THE COMPANY DEFINES THEM.

A customer relationship issue that has nothing to do with customer service is how the company will know the customers' definition of quality. It is often assumed that the company has sufficient insight into this to make gathering customer opinion and reaction data unnecessary. In many instances, this assumption does not hold.

A very visible example is the automotive industry. In the United States, automotive manufacturers have traditionally built the products they were absolutely and unwaveringly certain would suit the tastes of their buyers, while foreign competition has taken great chunks of the market by getting closer to real buyer values. In this blatant example, the U.S. motor companies managed to respond to the foreign competition, but only after the price of gasoline forced them to make some smaller cars. Then, ten years later, a large Detroit automaker under a remarkably visionary leader made great strides in quality. But his company seems to have let its quality slip considerably (especially in recently released models) since he retired. A posh British car maker provides another interesting case history. It sold flashy cars that were notoriously unreliable until a new managing director made his suppliers (notably the supplier of electrical parts) liable for parts returned under warranty. The company then made reliable cars for about eight years, and experienced a very large increase in sales, but is now slipping back into its former patterns. They assume their customers care more about sleek design and plush interiors than about reliability. All of the auto companies seem to think they know more about their customers' values than the customers do themselves, despite the clear lessons of the marketplace.

It is easy enough for any company to make this assumption erroneously. Most often the assumption is woven into the most basic theories of product differentiation and creative initiative. It is therefore difficult to challenge without losing the differentiation and innovation that forms the company's entire business strategy.

It is not uncommon to find that companies believe their customers ought to recognize the value of their product, because the product is something that the customer unquestionably needs and should therefore appreciate. However, needs do not always generate desires. This assumption, therefore, overlaps the previous one, that customers will always act in their best interest. They both assume that customers have a full appreciation of all of the factors related to the company's products, and a full grasp of their own values. This leads to the assumption that the customers' values will be the same ones that the company believes are best. Experience constantly proves otherwise. Market selection and product success are difficult at best to predict, forcing the conclusion that a business must be prepared to alter its views of value and quality based on the views of its customers.

ASSUMPTION 3.10
PERSONS RESPONSIBLE FOR CUSTOMER CONTACTS MUST KNOW ONLY THEIR IMMEDIATE JOBS AND HOW TO BEHAVE WITH CUSTOMERS.

Another way to state this assumption is that customer service representatives somehow automatically understand their company's workflow, or at least enough of it to help any customer with any problem. This is more often than not untrue. If a company is large enough, the odds are very good that no one knows all its work processes in detail. This assumption is one of the most subtle in the area of customer relationships, and the most frequently left unchallenged. The results are confusion, unfulfilled promises, and the appearance of chaos.

The ideal candidate for a position as a customer representative is, logically, someone very experienced in the workings of the company and completely familiar with the company's objectives for development. The customer service representative should also have a pleasing manner, and should be capable of finding the significant content in a possibly long-winded or confused discourse. A certain intelligence is required, as well as problem-solving capability and wit. With the addition of some basic financial acumen and the ability to create and communicate a vision for the company, the ideal customer service representative would make a very serviceable CEO. In practice, customer service personnel are often hired off the street and have no business experience, much less the required level of experience in the company itself. This is a matter of simple economics. However, their lack of experience can be and usually is addressed by intensive training, testing, and feedback. A company that is serious about client service will test its contacts frequently, thoroughly, and in detail. However, even the best service representative programs seldom include the company's business processes in their training. This is an unfortunate omission.

This single addition of training in corporate workflows would provide great benefits. Indeed, all of the customer contact personnel, including order clerks, could use this information to advantage. Not only would they be more informative, but they could also be more accurate in identifying problems, better able to predict outcomes, and better able to support the business in general. This is especially true for internal support processes, such as information technology, when the customers are internal company staff. A very effective set of possibilities for improvement of the entire functioning of the company is opened up when this assumption is challenged.

ASSUMPTION 3.11
THE COMPANY'S STAFF CONVEYS A SENSE OF URGENCY AND IMPORTANCE TO THE CUSTOMERS WITH WHOM THEY DEAL.

The most common complaint voiced by customers of companies that don't handle their customers very well is that the companies don't care about them. One of the cheapest and easiest ways to impress upon a customer that the company does in fact care is to convey a sense of urgency. Customers will never respect the company's response unless they are made to feel that they and their immediate business are important to the person who is communicating with them. Too often the assumption is made that customers are being handled this way, but this is seldom actually the case.

This is a customer contact requirement that is simply under-appreciated. Any company that examines its customer service and customer contacts will look for polite conduct and for responsiveness. They may go so far as to dictate a sequence of telephone responses to assure that the customer's entire requirement has been communicated and addressed. Then the assumption is made that if these two areas are covered, each contact will be successful. But what about those contacts that do not result in immediate satisfaction of a customer requirement? In those cases, and there will always be some, the customer will never be satisfied if no sense of urgency is conveyed. The contact will often end with the customer convinced that there is little chance the company will take any action at all. This wastes whatever time has been spent on that customer, and also invites another contact that will usually yield the same results, so there may be even more waste. If, however, the company's representative does succeed in conveying a sense of urgency, that may buy the time needed to address the customer's requirement while maintaining good will.

This is an important assumption to challenge, especially since customer service is such a substantial success factor. Conveying a sense of urgency may also spread to other areas of the company and have a positive impact on the basic productivity of the workforce.

CHALLENGING CUSTOMER RELATIONSHIP ASSUMPTIONS

There are two basic, widely known models of customer relations. The first, known as the "Sears Roebuck" model, is one in which a product or service is delivered or rendered immediately (or very quickly). When this is done, the customer does not need to know very much about the process being used by the company. They don't need to care. The other model is used when orders can't be delivered quickly. In these cases, the customer is told what the steps are, when they will happen, and when the finished product or service will be delivered. Generally, the final delivery date is only an estimate, but it is required to complete the customer's assurance of eventual satisfaction. This model works for large projects, and it is frequently used for internal work, such as computer program enhancements. In these cases, the promised intermediate dates must be met. It is also critical for this second model that everyone concerned, from operations to client services to the customer as well, knows the process in some detail. This model does not lend itself to surprises of any sort.

Once the customer service model has definitely been selected, challenging assumptions in this area is not difficult. Management can easily assess the quality of customer contacts just by emulating customers: calling their own customer service hot-lines and pretending to be distressed customers. This is the first step in challenging customer relationship assumptions. The second important step is evaluating the adequacy of the service staff. It is difficult to overcome the pressure to downsize the customer service staff, but it must be done. If there are insufficient customer contact personnel, there is very little hope of achieving good customer relations. The next step is to set specific customer relationship goals and measure the company's progress toward them. The fourth step is to open up more, not less, of the company to customer contact. Make every employee responsible for customer contact excellence.

From then on, the areas of improvement for customer relations are clearly established. First, all of the company's customer contacts must be managed, and managed aggressively. After having a potentially profitable product or service to offer, customer service is the most important function in business. Another well-known method used to strengthen this area is empowerment. Whenever possible, the customer's contact should have the authority and capability to satisfy the customer's requirement or solve the customer's problem. Finally, be sure that the contacts convey a sense of urgency to the customer. Customers must believe that their problem or desire is deemed to be of immediate importance to the company. Indeed, it should be.

Every contact with a customer is an opportunity. Hurrying the customer away, cutting costs at the customer's expense, or cutting back on customer service because it is believed that the customer will tolerate it, are worse than risky. Just don't do it.

MEASUREMENT: MANAGING THE BUSINESS OR JUST PLACING BLAME?

"MOST BUSINESS MEASUREMENTS ARE A SEARCH FOR BLAME."

Professor Stefano Sommadossi of Bocconi University in Milan captured the essence of measurement in business when he said that business measurements were established to identify trouble and to place the blame for it. Most measurement systems are intended to raise a red flag on exceptions to the company's operating plan, and for the most part negative ones. But effective measurement *is* indispensable in modern business.

Quantitative methods in business have gone through several trends in the past fifty years or so. Operations Research (OR), possibly the epitome of the use of numbers in enterprise, began in World War II, when of course it applied to military operations. When it began, OR was aptly named: every operations problem posed was researched by a team composed of various types of scientists, with support from mathematicians and statisticians. After the war, OR went into universities and into business, where it was slowly transformed into simply academic math applied to business. The founders of OR, such as C. West Churchman (who wrote, with Russell Akoff and E. Leonard Arnoff, OR's first textbook at the Case Institute of Technology in 1957), deplored the loss of the multidisciplined team; but schools must have a body of knowledge as their stock-in-trade, not just an effective approach to problem solving. The early 1960s saw numerical methods go wild in industry and government as formulas, computer models, and numerical planning methods raged unchecked under such thoroughly modern managers as Robert S. McNamara, who brought the Planning, Programming, and Budgeting system he pioneered at Ford into the Department of Defense and then to the World Bank. The methods worked well for him, but he was an exceptional manager with singular talents. McNamara could keep track of myriad details and still maintain sufficient perspective concerning what was important and what was not. The managers who followed him were not always able to do both. This is one of the paradoxes of numerical methods: management tends to apply its time and attention to areas that are easy to measure instead of areas that are significant to the business. In the 70s and 80s, increasing competition slowly turned management's attention back to the basics. Business had become saturated with numbers, but no magic had appeared in complex and voluminous numeric methods, so they quietly slipped into the background.

But all the thousands of formulas, algorithms, and little tricks that were developed in the numbers heyday remain in the books. Some of them are dredged up from time to time and put to use either as genuine attempts to solve problems or as cynical flummery in the hands of ambitious career seekers, unscrupulous consultants, and even a few counterfeit business school professors. There are indeed so many numerical approaches to business problems that it is difficult to count them.

GARBAGE IN, GARBAGE OUT

The Achilles heel of numerical analysis, however, is not the methods themselves but the raw data on which they are based. There are so many ways for good data to go bad that it is amazing when measurements actually turn out to be accurate. In business one usually finds that if there is a good way to analyze data to solve a pressing problem, either there is no method to get the right data at all, or if there is a method, it is already too late to apply it.

Today the use of data in business is at a relatively low ebb in terms of the funding given to executive information systems and in terms of business' reliance upon mathematics. The fad emphasizing numerical methods has, for the most part, subsided in terms of complexity and quantity, although more managers actually rely upon numbers today than in the past.

A good example of what has happened can be found in the common problem of inventory control. Mathematicians developed a formula for "economic order quantity" (EOQ). The optimal amount to order can be expressed as:

$$Q = \sqrt{\frac{2KM}{h}}$$

where Q is the right number to order per time period, K is a fixed setup cost, M is the number of items used in the time period, and h is the holding cost per unit. This is a fairly simple formula, but business has found an even better way. EOQ has largely been replaced by JIT (just-in-time.) Why have an inventory at all, some astute business people rightly asked? Mathematical precision was being applied blindly, under the unchallenged assumption that an inventory was required to keep production steady. By making special arrangements with suppliers, manufacturers can receive material just in time for production, thus transferring the burden of inventory to the supplier and requiring no formula at all.

While the extensive use of mathematical methods may not be missed by most business people, the business world is probably missing a bet by not doing more computer modeling. Some models were always respected for economic prediction, such as the Wharton Model, and some businesses, such as the oil industry and utilities, still rely heavily on modeling for their core business activities. Many business questions can be solved by modeling, but it requires an investment and years of support, making it unattractive to many executives today.

However, basic measurement for financial tracking and the assessment of operational performance has increased. The use of refined numerical methods by managers at every level in business amounts to a quiet revolution. But really effective use of numbers remains elusive.

In the past decade business seems to have developed a pattern for dealing with measurement. First, senior management becomes conscious that it is dissatisfied with what is being presented to it. They ask unit managers to come up with meaningful numbers to measure performance. Each business unit is to be responsible for defining what its significant outputs are, and how they should be measured. This first step usually fails. The business units generally offer to supply only information that shows them in a very good light, if they offer anything at all. Management's next step is to dictate the use of a set of performance metrics, generalized so that they apply across the entire business. If there is a consistent characteristic, these mandated measurements are mostly a way of deliberately looking for trouble: detecting performance below plan and finding some person or business unit to blame. The measurements are often gathered either by culling data from the company's computer systems or by having first-line managers fill out forms or spreadsheets. Executive staff pull together reports for a few years, but they are usually ignored after the first few quarters and then dropped after another reorganization.

NUMBERS DO COUNT

It doesn't have to be that way. Very effective managers use numbers extensively to make and support decisions. They rely upon metrics to tell them whether or not changes have been effective. Such managers, however, do not make invalid assumptions about the numbers they use. They do not assume that the data they are looking at are always accurate. They cross-check results and try several ways to approach measurement, and then they take the results with more than a grain of salt. They use real working data as the basis for their analyses. They understand whatever mathematics are used, and to assure understanding, they keep analysis simple whenever possible. Numbers are not only a benefit for a good business person, they are a requirement. But no assumptions are allowed to go unchallenged, because to do so is to allow the numbers to run the business. Effective managers just don't do that.

ASSUMPTION 4.1
ALL MEASUREMENTS ARE NEEDED. THE MORE MEASUREMENTS, THE MORE CONTROL.

Some businesses seem to be measurement-happy. If something moves, they measure it; if not, they measure it anyway. Their attitude is that the more metrics, the greater the control that management will have, not only over the work being done, but over all the factors that contribute to success. The only criterion for establishing a measurement is that a measurement can be made.

There are some obvious objections to doing business this way. The first is that there is certainly some wasted effort involved in measurement for its own sake. A more subtle problem is that management becomes lost in boiling geysers of data. The numbers become increasingly artificial, steering management's efforts in unproductive directions.

> One hapless company (and probably others) almost drove itself out of business by vigorously attacking a set of numerical goals that turned out to be poor indicators of success. The problem began with a bona fide self-improvement effort. Since the bottom line is a poor number to use to manage the operational details of any company, this company set up some more detailed performance targets, starting with sales. Gaining a new client was deemed the most important goal: who could argue with that in any business? The next most important sales goal was increasing sales to existing clients, on a client-by-client basis. The production organization measured itself by the units it produced, and the various ordering units measured the time it took to get an order into production. The time required to fill an order was not considered very important. In a few years, the company was fulfilling its goals, getting new clients and producing more products. All of the measurements looked good. However, the time required to ship orders was not being measured carefully, and it had become incredibly bad (some orders took four months to fill). Customers began to complain, return shipments, and go to the competition, usually in that order. It was true that the shipping time for their particular product was not always extremely important to most of their customers, but times over 60 days were usually intolerable, and in fact were not tolerated. Numbers were being used for management, but they were not the right numbers.

More often, when companies use too many numbers, some of them are just lost in the shuffle, badly reported, or not reported at all. It is common to pick a standard set of performance indicators for all parts of a business and then require each unit to interpret what they mean locally. When this is done, the numbers do not roll up meaningfully, but they are rolled up anyway. A good example of a common metric that is almost never useful is headcount. The number of employees is not a good gauge of staff expense. Managing by headcount almost invariably leads to the use of expensive temporary and contract staff. Another problem is that when a business reviews its measurement systems, it may add new metrics without deleting old ones. Newly appointed managers can also revise the meanings of performance metrics without telling anyone. Many measurement systems have become overly complex and irrelevant over decades of use, under the assumption that it is impossible to measure too much. But it is possible, even easy. Just don't do it.

ASSUMPTION 4.2
SOMEONE IS MEASURING THE RIGHT THINGS.

In a company that supports the traditional measurements, which include financial summaries (budget displayed against actual expense, with end-of-year extrapolated, and revenue displayed against plan, also calculated to end-of-year: all rolled up along organizational lines) and some performance figures, it is generally assumed that the lower levels of the business are measuring the things that they ought to be measuring in order to control their own operations. It is usually assumed that there are appropriate measures being used in most working-level units, and that because they vary from unit to unit, they cannot be rolled up or summarized for review at a higher level.

In most organizations there are few units really measuring their work independently, without having been specifically instructed to do so. Even these few naturally use measures that are intended to show the units in a favorable light. In some cases impressive numbers come out of units that the rest of the company would consider a dead waste of space and budget. There is some senior management awareness of this practice, but it is accepted nonetheless, based upon the assumption that somewhere else there are more appropriate measures being made that will show a true picture. This may or may not be happening.

There are also many cases in which measurements are in fact being made, but not reported outside the unit making them. Occasionally, key measurements are made, recorded, and even entered in a computer, but not actually used for any purpose. A large financial institution discovered in a recent business process improvement project that a form they were using was counted by every unit that touched it, but the tallies were never checked against each other nor used as performance indicators—indeed they were not used at all. Not only was effort being wasted, but there were no checks on the possible loss or delay of the form while it was being processed. Everyone involved thought someone else was keeping track of the numbers.

This is an easily challenged assumption, once it is discovered.

ASSUMPTION 4.3
FIGURES ON REPORTS ARE USUALLY CORRECT ENOUGH TO USE.

Most business people distrust the numbers that are presented to them in almost any situation. They are not able to tell precisely where the numbers come from, what they include and what they don't, and what the timing of reporting them is. Despite this skepticism, the assumption is almost always made that the numbers on a report are accurate enough for whatever use is intended at the moment. Sometimes this assumption is warranted, sometimes it is not.

Within the purview of accounting there is a certain amount of protection afforded to the users of numbers by law and generally accepted accounting principles. Even these protections can fail, however, producing misleading results from time to time. In some international venues, the protection of accounting practices is not completely reliable. Here is an example.

> A few years ago, when Turkey first tried to join the common market, their accounting practices impeded their attempt. In Turkey, there were no rules for aggregating financial information, so some of the large conglomerates moved money around and showed an overall increase that should have been washed out. The large conglomerates all owned banks that would routinely lend money to industrial companies in the same conglomerate, showing both the cash that had been transferred as an asset in the borrower company, and the debt as an asset in the bank. This practice confused even Turkish investors, who relied more on inside information than on published reports.

Outside of the accounting profession, there is no legal control over numbers, and almost anything can happen to them. Generally the problems are not caused by misleading practices so much as by number-hungry staff grabbing whatever looks like an applicable metric, not knowing how it came to be wherever they found it. As automated support for business grows increasingly complex, it becomes increasingly difficult to determine just where a number in a database comes from, when and how it is updated, who has access to it, and whether or not it has ever been verified against reality. It is sometimes troublesome to do the research required to verify the numbers that appear on reports, but it should be done when a number is to be used for a new purpose. It is easier to assume that the numbers are good enough, but they may not be. Just don't do it.

ASSUMPTION 4.4
IF THERE IS A NUMBER REPORTED, MANAGEMENT IS IN CONTROL OF WHAT IS BEING MEASURED.

This may be the most damaging assumption related to numbers in business. When it is a false assumption, as it often is, a company's future may be in jeopardy.

The view from the top of the company is a set of numbers, generally expenses and revenues rolled up along organizational lines. There is a corporate bottom line for which the CEO is responsible; the next level of detail is a series of figures for each major business unit, usually under a senior vice president or, for very large companies, a division president. Each of these managers is required to assume responsibility for the performance of a business unit. This would not seem to be an assumption, but a mandated and tested obligation. However, after a few quarters, the members of a new management team who have been successful in delivering their numbers are assumed to be in control of them. The assumption is only questioned when the numbers are not achieved, by which time it may be too late.

In recent years there has been a high turnover in CEOs. This problem is due to the increased demands that competition has placed on business. The second level of senior management is almost as volatile. A new CEO will typically bring new people into the next tier in all areas where there are visible problems. A new CEO may base the decision to retain an existing vice president on a combination of the VP's numerical success and the impressions that the CEO gets in interviewing the old managers and high-level staff. So new vice presidents often find themselves in charge of areas that have specific shortfalls: shortfalls betrayed by the area's numbers. But the new VPs often manage to negotiate reasonable targets for the first year or so, targets that can be reached by simply putting pressure on underlings and doing a bit of trimming at the margin. They do not need to gain real control over their numbers for several years, by which time the overall situation of the business may well have changed. The VPs who are not new manage more stable areas, and they too are not really tested in numerical combat. Therefore, volatile business conditions have placed increasing emphasis on numbers, but have paradoxically not produced a generation of managers who are really in command of them.

ASSUMPTION 4.5
INTERNAL AUDIT KNOWS BEST. THE CONTROLS THEY RECOMMEND TO MEASURE PERFORMANCE AND EFFICIENCY ARE ALL NECESSARY.

To justify its jobs, internal audit feels it must come up with recommendations, sometimes marginal ones, and then back them as being critical to the company's security and integrity. The assumption is often made that these recommendations are ineluctable. In process improvement projects, it is very common to find the root of a highly inefficient activity in a long-forgotten internal audit report. These recommendations should be taken only with a grain of salt, and should be energetically opposed if the recommendation seems unnecessary. Much wasted motion will naturally grow over the years otherwise.

Here is an example of an audit recommendation that was not accepted. Unfortunately, most are implemented because it is too much trouble to resist.

One internal auditor was assigned to audit the computer facility of a large bank. Having no previous experience with computer facilities, the auditor was alarmed when the Halon fire extinguishing system's operation was described. It is a tradition among computer center staff everywhere to describe the Halon system in a dramatically alarming manner; they do it to everyone who tours their facilities. Halon is an inert gas that can smother an electrical fire by being deployed with almost explosive force. It displaces all the air in the computer room in a few seconds. It is annoying to be in a computer room when Halon deploys, perhaps even frightening, but it is not dangerous, although some of the ceiling tiles will probably be blown out and scattered all over the room. The noise is truly horrifying. But the gas is not poisonous, and there is a loud warning alarm before the Halon is released.

Due to the expense of refilling the compressed Halon cylinders, these systems are never fully tested, nor demonstrated for visitors. The auditor was very concerned about the safety of the computer room staff, probably due to their dramatized description of how the system worked. The result was a recommendation to procure gas masks for the computer room. This was laughed off at first, but the auditor stuck to the recommendation, and it was necessary to get a written statement from the local fire marshal stating that the gas masks represented a greater danger to the staff than the Halon in order to close the recommendation. Some companies would have bought the gas masks.

The same skepticism that was applied to the issue of gas masks by the bank should be applied to audit recommendations that require new measurements and checks on production. Accept only good audit recommendations. The others may seem like only minor nuisances when considered one by one, but over time they may add up to an inefficient operation.

ASSUMPTION 4.6
THE COMPANY'S MEASUREMENT SYSTEM INSURES THAT NOTHING GETS LOST.

There are companies that tell themselves: "We track everything." These companies usually do try to track everything and, although few succeed in doing so, the question of why never arises. It is also often questionable that everything is really tracked fully, but that question is usually moot compared to the issue of whether or not the effort is relevant.

This assumption is difficult to challenge. It is usually set deeply in the attitudes and work habits of management and staff. It also sounds reasonable. For example, there would certainly be dire consequences if a company made a habit of losing orders. However, copies of orders may not require as much protection, and if there are several copies in the company, the chances of losing all of them are remote. The costs of tracking paper, however, are very great. Sometimes it is worth taking a business risk of losing an important transaction once in a blue moon (or perhaps never) to cut costs dramatically.

An interesting experiment can be conducted to prove this point. Take a document and hide it. See if there is any negative result, or if a copy is found somewhere and the entire cost of the lost document turns out to be a slight delay and a few cents for a photocopy.

ASSUMPTION 4.7
POST-PROCESS PRODUCTION MEASUREMENTS INSURE QUALITY.

Experts in quality have always known that post-production testing may be able to measure quality, but it cannot improve it. There is a business assumption that just measuring an activity will result in the beginnings of improvement. This assumption seems reasonable often enough to give it credibility, and it often actually happens. Indeed, any attention to an activity may improve it. There is a common story (it seems to have happened in many businesses) about an experiment in office lighting. Two areas of a large building were monitored for performance. One had its lighting increased, the other did not. The performance of both areas improved. It was not the lighting, but the knowledge that they were being monitored that improved the performance of both groups. However, quality does not appear to obey this principal. Just measuring quality does not improve it.

In the early 1960s, the Society for Nondestructive Testing put out a comical pamphlet for one of its meetings that defined "inspection" as "the process that quality cannot be gotten into products by means of which." The fact that inspection could not provide quality was so well known even in those pre-Deming days as to be a catchphrase.

Quality is actually "gotten" into products and services by actively improving the processes that produce them, not by simply observing them, not even when the observation is quantified and certainly not after the process has ended. But the assumption persists, especially in service industries (newcomers that they are to manufacturing's long battle to improve quality). Service industries have historically used accounting as their numerical measure of success, with quality equating to financial accuracy. Financial accuracy is certainly a quality issue, but it is far from being the only component of service quality. Furthermore, financial accuracy is usually measured using methods that positively cannot work for the delivery of the service itself.

Industrial examples of this problem abound, but there is a particularly interesting one in financial services.

The company produced a service that was subject to external audit. To provide some measure of protection, the company had implemented an internal post-processing audit that was performed on a randomly selected sample of about ten percent of the completed services. The auditor identified problems, and each problem was charged to the staff who worked on the services in which the problems were found. These reports directly affected the performance reviews of the staff. Naturally, there were differences of opinion over marginal situations. Management was forced to play a double role, backing their staff while supporting audit's protection of the company. The attention of the entire staff became focused on the auditors, rather than on improving quality. Audit personnel entered and left the building through different doors from the other staff, and they ate lunch in separate groups, presumably in fear of physical attack.

After years of strife, a friendly, in-line audit was placed in the process. The back-end audit was cut down in size and the auditors were rotated. The cooperative effort improved quality dramatically, since the friendly auditors were able to influence the quality of services and to teach the staff directly to avoid problems. However, it should be noted that the real improvement came from the staff, not the auditors. Quality is a function of process and staff, not of any form of inspection or audit.

ASSUMPTION 4.8
INTANGIBLES, LIKE QUALITY, CANNOT BE MEASURED.

Some of business' most important objectives are not measured because they are assumed to be intangible, which means that they are soft, untouchable, and unmeasurable. The most common of these is quality, but there are many others, such as customer satisfaction, morale, risks of all sorts, and the contribution of an individual person to the company's growth objectives. This is one of the reasons that businesses waste time on irrelevant measurements while important ones are often neglected.

We cannot overemphasize: *there is almost always a way to quantify so-called intangibles.* Opinion variables, such as perceived quality, can be surveyed and graded on any given scale, so long as it is consistent. Experts in the measurement of behavior have studied scales and advise that a one-to-five scale is as effective as most finer divisions, since most people cannot readily subdivide their opinions beyond five levels. Many difficult metrics can be made easier to measure by just quantifying the change from one time period to another, rather than by setting an absolute scale. Sometimes measurements are not numeric at all, but are other reliable, repeatable indicators, such as a total absence of complaints. It often requires creativity to invent a such a metric, but there really is no such thing as an important business objective that cannot be subjected to appropriate measurement.

There is a story, perhaps legend is a better word, about snow removal in Denver that illustrates the use of creative ways to set objectives.

Over twenty years ago, Denver's public works organization was severely criticized for its failure to remove snow effectively. They looked at other cities and even engaged professional consultants, but to no avail. There were limited resources, and no good way to allocate them. Finally, a group from the nearby Colorado School of Mines was asked to look at the problem. First, they asked for a map of the city showing all the streets. Then they asked the public works staff to mark the map with the homes of each member of the city council. They next drew routes from the council's homes to the city center. They advised public works to clear those routes first. They solved the problem. It was not just a political trick; the council members were, of course, distributed among the city's geographically distributed voting districts. The solution was equitable, it provided connections from all of the neighborhoods in the city, and it was also politically astute. They did this without using any mathematics, but the principles were those of a logical approach to an organizational problem, which is the underlying reason for the use of numbers and mathematics in business.

An intangible that is often overlooked and yet is quite measurable is the degree of consensus in a business over some of its pressing issues. Consensus management, as is pointed out in Chapter 8, "Just Don't Rely on Consensus Management," is so riddled with political overtones as to hinder any business. But measuring the actual opinions of junior managers when they are forced to tell the truth can be very interesting to senior managers. Polling of opinions and even carefully controlled consensus building can be done by the Delphi Method, a numerical method that was invented at the RAND Corporation in 1948 for predicting the future of technology. Delphi uses controlled voting, in which the issues are clarified and voted on anonymously in successive rounds. In each round, all of the participants are allowed a vote (usually on a one-to-five scale) and one line of commentary, if desired. The unique features of Delphi are (according to N.C. Dalkey, of the RAND Corporation): (1) anonymity, (2) controlled feedback, and (3) statistical group response. The use of the Delphi approach for consensus building was pioneered at Case Western Reserve University in work headed by Professor Burton Dean. One of the best sources of information about the Delphi method is an article in the May, 1970 issue of *Business Week* entitled "Forecasters Turn to Group Research." Delphi is but one of many approaches by which intangibles can be effectively quantified for use in business decision making. The assumption that there is no way to do this is very nearly always wrong.

CHALLENGING THE ASSUMPTIONS OF QUANTITATIVE METHODS IN BUSINESS

Clearly and simply stated, it is a demonstrable necessity of modern business that if it is not in the numbers, it does not exist. Everything must come down to a quantitative representation. This is a beneficial result of the financial perspective that has dominated business for the past several decades. Because of this fact, numeric presentation and justification are critical. Metric systems have two main purposes: they prove a point or they provide decision-related information. If the numbers do not prove the point, it will not be accepted. If the numbers in a monitoring metric system are not able to alert management, they can be a real danger to the company. The methods and metric systems that are used provide credibility and justification. Where standard corporate metric systems are in place, they must be used or proven false. Where no system is in place to provide the necessary numeric presentation, a customized one must be invented. But, in any custom metric system, concurrence and acceptance must be achieved. The only valid use of any metric system is to prove a point. If the system leaves room for argument or disagreement it is less than worthless. Proving a point should not be an invitation to challenge. If it is, the point is lost before it is made.

While the metric system that is used must provide repeatable, accurate results, the assumptions that serve as the system's foundation should be open to discussion. If the assumptions are conservative, the probability of their being readily accepted, and the numbers reported under them believed, is high, and should remain so. However, it is safest to make sure the system is acceptable to all who will use it before trying to implement it, no matter how obvious its assumptions seem.

Many of the metric systems in use today are old and very changeable. Many are based on layered sets of controls and checks that are not applicable in today's automated environment. Similarly, many of the base numbers that are obtained must also be challenged. They are the results of metric systems that are designed to prove specific points. These points may be in conflict with today's business operation and may simply be based on irrelevant or incorrect assumptions, when applied to the present business operation. The key in selecting, creating, or using a metric system is thus plausibility. Is it reasonable? Is it logical? Is it simple? Yes, simple. Complex metric systems are viewed with distrust. Error probability is also much higher in complex systems. While most managers today have a firm understanding of business arithmetic, very few are mathematicians. The key is understandability, so simple is always best.

The second key in a metric system is that it must be comprehensive, or the picture it gives to management will be incomplete. In many companies, metric systems have been so narrowly focused that they failed to take into account the essential interrelationships between groups. Finally, the third key requirement for metric systems is accuracy, the need for which is obvious.

FIRST STEPS IN CHALLENGING METRIC SYSTEMS

Once attention is focused on the problem, the methods used to challenge measurement assumptions are easily understood and applied. This application is unfortunately more often avoided than not. Most managers fear the complexity of their company's current metric systems and, of course, they are also reluctant to seem lacking in mathematical ability. Many managers are also reluctant to discuss challenging metrics because they may seem to have poor control of their own numbers. In too many cases, managers actually have very little control over their own metrics.

Starting to challenge the assumptions of measurement begins with the simple question: "Do we measure the right things to help all of the people in the company do their work well?" A good time to say no to this question is when the business has not honestly assessed its metrics recently. Metrics must change with changes in the business, and should be designed when changes are first planned. If there have been changes in organization, management approach, or process in the firm's recent history, measurements should at least have been reviewed. If they weren't, this is a good time to do it.

The first rule of business measurement is to avoid "report-only" measurements. These are numbers that are not actually used by the organizations reporting them; they are put together only to placate management. All measurements reported to management should be the ones actually used by those who report them for controlling their own work. Any report-only measurement should be treated with suspicion. The second important factor of metrics is that they be immediately relevant and representative, not just convenient. A performance metric should measure precisely what the company expects the individual or unit to contribute to the business, or it will motivate a misalignment of effort. Third, measurement should be looked upon as an aid to working, not as an instrument of blame. W. Edwards Deming advised management to "drive fear out" of business processes, and making measurements more friendly is a key step in that direction. Deming is also a good source for meaningful business metrics; much of his work, famous for his 14 principles of quality improvement, was quantitative. He proved that quality can always be measured, and that it should be.

Another way to challenge the measurement system is to simply reduce the quantity of numerical information that is used in management. Keep only the important metrics. Any business can become data-rich and information-poor if the quantity of management information is not carefully controlled.

A good place to look for appropriate measurements is in change projects, especially business process improvement and reengineering projects. When process is analyzed, targeted activity outputs can be identified, measured, and compared. This provides several benefits, including the essential ability to evaluate the effectiveness of the change project, as well as a basis for activity-based measurement systems. These can complement the long-standing practices of financial accounting, which are in fact best restricted to their original intention of tracking monetary transactions. Financial numbers are not very good indicators of performance, except of course for the entire company. The business's financial numbers are certainly the best place to look for trend analysis, since they are likely to be the only numbers that have been gathered consistently over a long period of time. But accounting should not be looked on as the only group in the business that can manage numbers. Numbers are an important part of every manager's job. Their importance can only increase as business becomes more complex and more competitive.

THE ROLE OF METRICS IN DEFINING THE STRATEGY OF THE COMPANY

As companies move into the future, metric systems that address the users, their values, and their patterns should be created. In his book, *The Death of Competition,* James Moore writes convincingly about "business ecosystems" and "co-evolving" groups of companies, suppliers, customers, and competitors. The aggregation of business segments into ecosystems and the creation of new relationships with companies in various places in the world will require a very different set of metric systems from those that companies have used in the past. These systems themselves will evolve and must be controlled through a more comprehensive process that we call "evolutive management." (See Chapter 2, "Just Don't Tolerate Business As Usual," for more about evolutive management.)

In several books that deal with defining the strategies of companies, two themes are always mentioned: 1) the need to break the molds of the past and 2) the need to include the ideas of a greater range of personnel than just the managing committee and board of directors. The problem in doing either of these is that strategic "brainstorming" can create infeasible concepts. The determining factors must be related to new metric systems—metric systems that have largely not yet been created. The need to mold new, more creative metric systems requires an imagination that many companies lack or are afraid to explore. Breaking with tradition is difficult.

At this point it seems clear that the metric systems of the future will be highly individualized. Commonly used systems of the past will not continue to serve the changing needs of business. The future systems will be based on new principles, such as value-based evaluation, discussed in Chapter 9.

Weakness in the corporate metric system is a serious failing. In tomorrow's successful company, an arsenal of sound metrics about the operation and the market will be an indispensable tool. These systems will provide a clear picture of both the present and the most potentially viable and profitable future strategy. And the numbers will be understood by every employee in the company.

THE HUMAN ASSET

IN ITS SIMPLEST TERMS, MANAGEMENT
MEANS ACHIEVEMENT THROUGH THE
EFFORTS OF OTHER PEOPLE.

A company is by definition a group of people organized to achieve a common goal. Every business is such a group. It would seem obvious that the human side of enterprise would naturally receive management's primary attention. But today those at the working levels of business view corporate management with mistrust. Rightly or not, many workers believe that management has broken faith with them. Many who have been loyal for years, often having made sacrifices for the company, have found themselves suddenly threatened with being downsized or cut back. Business appears to have lost any sense of obligation to its employees.

All levels of management, however, agonize over staffing, more today than ever before. Competition forces decisions upon managers that they do not want to make. Managers believe that their concern for their employees is (and appears) unabated, and that every possible alternative is exercised before they reduce staff. Although management is not surprised that the working staff fear these reductions, they do find some of the visible reactions of employees inappropriate. Management believes that employees should work harder to compete for their existing jobs. Managers feel that increased efforts will avoid the need to reduce the company's payroll, and that this will be obvious to all employees. In this their hopes have been disappointed.

Management's opinion is that staff now lack loyalty and dedication. Staff often seem sullen and without the willingness to do what is needed to get the job done. This attitude appears to some managers to be getting worse. Some have become cynical, and react to all staff complaints with the prevailing retort: "With all the cutbacks, you should be glad you have a job."

While almost all employees are glad they have a job, and most feel that the company attaches some value to their work, they believe the company is willing to ignore their experience and competencies if there is any trouble. So their willingness to go the extra mile for the good of the company has been severely impacted. There is simply little or no trust left.

A great many senior workers believe that their value to the company will actually become a danger to them if there are mass staff cuts. Employees of the longest standing have the highest salaries and also the greatest claim on the company retirement funds. On the other hand, the less experienced staff feel that they are the easiest to get rid of, having no friends and less experience than their seniors. So everyone just waits and worries, believing that they are not protected from a reduction. Even in companies that have not downsized, the workforce is often skeptical—many of them have friends or family members who have lost their jobs. The belief that a person can work for a single company for an entire career and then be taken care of has been destroyed. As evidenced by the rate of staff and management turnover, people are placing less and less importance on a long-term relationship with a company. Workers do not believe a long-term relationship will happen.

Many workers feel that they are under greater pressure today than at any time in the past. This pressure is not imaginary. The need to get the work done with fewer workers (or, more precisely, with a lower labor cost) is very real. But the mass reduction in force is a crude and ineffective approach to reducing the costs of products and services. An arbitrary cut in staff may actually have a damaging effect on productivity. Mass layoffs do not rid a company of its dead wood in most cases. More often than not, the best people leave at the first hint of a downsizing. These people are the most marketable and they do not want to take a chance on the downsizing roulette wheel. Long-term workers are usually given early retirement options, and they generally accept them. The result is that the company is left with a concentration of the people it really wants to lose. Therefore, when the good and long-term workers are gone, the company inevitably winds up having to keep many people who should have been released.

While this practice of the past several years does unquestionably meet short-term financial goals and it can give an immediate boost to the company's stock, it has proven to be both disruptive and destructive. Generally, in companies that downsize, absenteeism, stress, and anxiety-related problems all go up, but the willingness of the workforce to make the company succeed goes down.

Depression and other visible evidence of discontent are becoming common. Discontentment is like an iceberg: only the top is visible. The biggest part of the rift between management and workers is submerged out of sight. But it has the potential to have a more severe impact on business. The hidden dangers in mass staff reductions are negative attitude and lack of commitment. Many workers and managers have developed hostile attitudes, and commitment to their jobs is minimal. The worst effect is the recent development of an irreconcilably defensive attitude toward management. The combined effect is a deterioration of effectiveness and productivity. Thus, although money is being saved on the balance sheet, the ability of the company to improve or even maintain past levels of quality and efficiency have often been seriously eroded.

CHANGING TIMES, CHANGING WORK ETHIC

This trend is also reflected in the young people entering the workforce. The work ethic has changed. Fewer young people are willing to give the time and loyalty their parents gave to their jobs. Many people today have haunting memories of living through family disruption as close relatives were cast out of their jobs. The result is a lack of willingness to commit themselves to an organization that they believe will fire them for the least financial advantage, even if they are doing a great job.

Another casualty of downsizing is the delicate balance between unions and management. This problem is resulting from the deteriorating relationship between the workforce and management in many companies. One of its manifestations is the extension of unionization into the ranks of middle management in some companies. Clearly, wherever people feel that management is making arbitrary or unfair decisions, the unions will eventually become involved.

THE MORE WITH LESS MYTH

The single biggest problem with many of the cutbacks we have seen has been a lack of work restructuring. Cuts are most often driven by financial considerations, not by work requirements. It is assumed that there must be "fat" in the operation and that the managers will cut the excess. However, if there is excess staffing, it usually does not take the form of many excess people. Unused person-power is usually distributed among many people. The only way to cut this sort of "fat" is to redistribute the work. To be successful, work redistribution requires that the work flow be changed. This is done through reengineering, not mass reductions in force. But in most cases, the cutbacks have been arbitrary, based on senior management's opinion, rather than on any real knowledge. Only in very few cases have the cutbacks been based on the real relationship between the work and the workforce.

Unless work restructuring occurs, the same amount of work will be needed both before and after the cutback. There are no actual gains in efficiency or effectiveness realized from staff cutting alone. With fewer people, the survivors have no choice but to absorb the work of the departed staff as best they can or to cut out entire functions. In many companies the staff has reached its saturation point and there is no flexibility to absorb more work, so cutting out tasks is often the result. Special projects and important improvement functions are usually the first to go. They are simply put on the back burner, destined to remain there indefinitely. With no improvement projects, there is little hope of doing the work better with fewer people. The situation is common in U.S. businesses: no progress is being made, and major divisions and even whole companies are essentially treading water.

Some companies are even worse off. Another major problem that has resulted from the downsizing of the past several years is the disruption of the organization and in some cases the inability of the company to continue to operate. Many companies assumed that their managers would know *who* to let go as percentage cuts released large numbers of people. But history has now shown that this assumption was flawed. Managers did not always know who to lay off. In many cases, people the company relied on were cut. In some cases the operations virtually ground to a halt. It is not news that companies have been forced to hire back key staff at all levels as "consultants," at several times their old salaries.

While we now know that percentage cutbacks do not work, companies continue to allow short-term financial objectives—cut staff to cut costs—to guide staffing.

This is not just an American problem. In Japan, where employees had long-held expectations of being taken care of, companies are now deciding on layoffs and cutbacks. In Europe many companies are rethinking the age-old practice of giving workers most of August off. Clearly, a new era of staff relations is about to dawn; the question is what will that era look like? Will it be driven by long-range planning or by short-term financial goals?

THE DECIMATION OF MIDDLE MANAGEMENT

Cutbacks and downsizing have undoubtedly increased workloads to the breaking point in many companies. The knowledge workers have often been hit as hard as the unskilled. The result is that fewer people know how to do studies, evaluations, and operation redesign. Change management is thus more difficult. The problem is that if one assumes the company will stay in business, the hiring and training of new knowledge workers will create a delay in the company's ability to respond to immediate opportunities or even long-term ones in a timely manner.

Fear seems to rule all levels of staff and management in many organizations. While this fear is nothing new to the unskilled workers, it is new to the skilled and middle managers. Everyone is waiting for the proverbial ax to fall, and wondering if they will be the next victims. The concept of the flat organization is showing its inherent weaknesses in many corporations. Some managers have a direct span of control over 20 or 30 people. Without the successful installation of self-directed teams, which doesn't always work, these managers have no hope of doing anything other than listening to people's problems.

RIDING THE TURNOVER SPIRAL TO MEDIOCRE PERFORMANCE

There is a destructive pattern emerging in business, based upon the instability of management positions. Most studies of management turnover put the general tenure of a manager in any position at two to three years. The good news is that the workforce is very mobile and there is a ready pool of presumably well-trained managers and knowledge workers to choose from. The bad news is that any mobile force tends to be mercenary in nature and that the past concepts of loyalty, security, and retirement are no longer valid. Most managers do, in fact, recognize and show some concern for the best interests of the company they work for, provided that their personal interests are not threatened or compromised in some way. Most of the management turnover is caused by reorganization and promotion, but there is still a high rate of managers quitting their companies for apparently greener pastures.

A key force in the behavior of management is frustration. Many managers and knowledge workers find the pace of decision making and business improvements so slowed by staff reductions and falling budgets as to be incompatible with their personal ambitions. In many companies, these people feel that nothing is getting done and that their contributions have no value. This frequently causes the best people in the company to move on.

Regardless of why a manager leaves, excessive turnover is occurring. The real problem is that this turnover results in little or no accomplishment. While work gets done and product gets out, nothing new happens and little improvement occurs. In fact, there is a cycle that one can see in most companies.

Assuming that a managerial position is filled and that person has been in that job for about a year to a year and a half, we now see a change occurring. The managers are becoming mired in politics, or have not gotten what they think is fair treatment, or have not had the support they had thought was agreed to when they were hired, or any one of dozens of problems is causing them to fear for their jobs. The result is that many managers start thinking about moving more quickly now than at any time in the past.

The manager now enters the next phase, the treading water state. Once this phase is arrived at, the manager virtually stops all forward movement. Nothing seems worth the effort. After all, they will be leaving soon anyway so why bother to work themselves to death. Projects are either delayed indefinitely, canceled, or just given lip service. The daily operation continues to churn out whatever it produces, minor problems are addressed, budgets are prepared, plans are made, but nothing really gets done other than the daily status quo. Projects that are approved and funded languish, new initiatives are publicly supported but not included in the operation's work, and useless meetings become the norm. This state continues until the person is moved, gets fired, or finds a new position—usually at least eight months.

When the manager leaves, the operation now has no head, and all lower-level managers shut down, waiting for the inevitable appointment of a new leader and the change that always comes with new management. The interim manager does not want to make waves and works mainly at being friendly and politicking for the job. New work is viewed as risky and generally nothing of any substance is started—certainly not if the interim manager has any choice. Even vacancies in critical lower-level positions are left open. The excuse is that no one wants to begin any effort until the new "boss" comes on board because they don't know what he will want to do or how she will want to organize the activity. Similarly, no new people are hired (aside from very low-level people) because the new boss should have the right to choose all his or her people. This is the no-change state for a business unit. As it can take a long time to find the right new manager, this state can last up to eight months or more. Meetings intensify during this period and fighting increases as tensions mount, but the result is always continued stagnation. The longer this state lasts, the more disruptive it becomes as less and less gets done.

Then a new manager is selected, usually to begin work about a month after being appointed. Now the unit goes into a state of complete shutdown—nothing at all happens. Virtually everything, including many daily activities, shuts down as everyone spends all their time rumoring about the new boss and what he or she will want, be like, and do. This frantic speculating can affect everyone in the operation, as they wonder about downsizing and other actions new managers take to make a good first impression on their managers.

When the new manager finally arrives, there is a frenzied level of activity, but no real work, as the entire staff tries to seem very busy. The amount of "make-work" skyrockets. Virtually everything but making the widget has stopped for many months in anticipation of finding a new top manager for the operation. Now everyone feels they must look productive and must be working on something important. But there are no real projects underway.

This continues until the new manager gets his or her feet wet, and has some basic understanding of the operation. The manager who is eager to make an impression usually acts quickly to take some drastic action to improve everything. This is often premature and causes more harm than good. Timid managers keep everything shut down, because they don't want to do the wrong thing. Good managers are somewhere in the middle. But, regardless, this state of "chaos" will last for up to seven or eight months.

After the initial shakeout is completed, the manager and staff can get down to the business of improving the operation. This is the beginning of the productive state. Depending on the average turnaround time, this state will last up to a year before the manager begins to question his or her longevity in the position, becomes bored, becomes disenchanted, or thinks he or she can do better somewhere else. At that point, the operation goes back into a no-change state.

The result is that out of every three years a company can expect about one year of really productive work, work toward improvement or the achievement of goals. Of course this is a generalization, but in many companies and for many managers it is not far from accurate. The question is not whether this situation exists, but rather how it can be changed.

ASSUMPTIONS THAT MUST ALWAYS BE CHALLENGED

The assumptions in this chapter address issues and habits that we find in most companies. They are often politically sensitive and they represent attitudes and practices that have often become so ingrained into corporate thinking that no one even considers them any longer. But, like many things that are just taken for granted, many no longer fit into the culture needed to move forward. We have challenged these assumptions in many of our client companies and we have found that significant improvements in productivity, effectiveness, and personnel relations can be gained from asking the questions that will naturally be part of any evaluation.

Interestingly, we find that these evaluations trigger others as managers learn about the way management and human resources (HR) policy really function in companies. Clearly, there is room for improvement. The way to start is by questioning the following assumptions.

ASSUMPTION 5.1
EMPLOYEES WILL MAKE THE COMPANY'S OBJECTIVES THEIR OWN.

Many managers at all levels assume that the goals of the company are the only accepted goals of all its managers and staff. It is further assumed that these goals are correctly described by each level of management to the managers and staff below them.

While this may be an accurate assumption for some very small companies, it is not true in larger ones. In small companies, everyone believes they are in the same boat and everyone knows that unless they pull together, the boat will sink and they will pay the price—personally. In large companies, few managers or staff believe that they can contribute to the decline of the company. Some few believe that they can contribute to its success, but few believe that they can actually cause a problem.

The real problem is thus in larger companies. In these operations, managers frequently have their own agendas. These can vary widely, but all affect the way the person will look at any goal or any change, causing a redefinition of the goal in terms of the operation and the organization unit. Because most companies rely on "word of mouth" to carry the goals to most levels of managers, the intent and meaning of the goals undergo many individually subtle changes as they move from level to level.

The result is a disconnection of the operation from senior management. This disconnection is often fairly well hidden. Everyone is using the same terms and on the surface everything seems to be working fine. But goals are not really met and over time the operation becomes out of tune. Coordination is difficult and isolation seems to prosper as managers build walls of noncooperation around themselves.

Unfortunately, these walls are often supported by planning, budgeting, and evaluation activities. Managers must fight for their budgets, to the detriment of those who stand in their way. Managers must also show how their operations will support the corporate plan—as they interpret it. Of course a manager's plan and budget are closely tied to justifying the position taken in support of the manager's game plan. For example, if cutting the budget will gain the manager recognition, the budget will be cut. If compensation is tied to staff size and scope of responsibility, the manager will be motivated to justify additional staff. "Turf wars" often exist in this type of corporate environment.

Because one would generally think that anything that is good for the company is good for the managers and workers, it is most often believed that people will do what is best for the company: it is in their best interest to do so. Unfortunately, this model is breaking down. People often have little belief in their tenure with any company. Many managers and knowledge workers have become very concerned about their marketability and focus on the things that may be done to increase their own career options. While this is not necessarily detrimental if it can be channeled inward, the common situation is that people move up by moving out of the company. The result is that people often interpret plans and take actions that they perceive to be in their best interest, but these interests may not be in alignment with those of the company. Indeed the interests of individual managers may be diametrically opposed to the interests of the business as a whole.

ASSUMPTION 5.2
JUST CUT PAYROLL COSTS AND THE BOTTOM LINE
WILL IMPROVE.

In past years, the majority of downsizing and staff adjustments have been based on budget cuts. The basis for these cuts is usually either the selection of an arbitrary percentage (or payroll dollar amount) or the elimination of entire business units. With the advent of the short-term and shortsighted financial objective and the drive to cut costs, people are increasingly being thought of only as a liability on the balance sheet. Any distinction by skill or knowledge is seldom made. Too many companies consider employees only in terms of their loaded salaries. The value of an individual is calculated in terms of the savings their termination will subtract from the expense report. Performance appraisals and other key worth indicators are simply not considered.

Although many of these cost reduction efforts achieve their target numbers, the resulting impact on the company is not always what senior management had in mind. While it is generally assumed that any reduction in cost is good, the reality is that when cost reduction is driven improperly and by arbitrary goals, the results can be disruptive. We have seen many cases where key functional support has been inadvertently eliminated. Key knowledge workers have been lost and with the general lack of up-to-date written procedures in most companies, the irreplaceable knowledge and backgrounds of these people are lost. The result is a fairly rapid deterioration of the operation. Things just stop working. The example on the next page is presented courtesy of Richard Borgo, of the RGB Group, located in Crystal Lake, Illinois.

The need to reduce costs is very real but, when implemented on a percentage basis or in a hurry, the results can be surprising. Clearly, when cuts are required, a detailed understanding of the business operation is needed. Our experience has been that few companies have a detailed understanding of who does what and when or why. In the absence of this information, companies have had no other option but to cut across the board. But with the introduction of process mapping and work flow analysis, many companies now have the type of information, if they model the current

A natural resource provider wanted to improve the bottom line by reducing operating costs through the reduction of its administrative personnel. As part of this reduction, senior management mandated the implementation of voice mail. All duties of the individual secretaries were then assigned to one departmental secretary. Most of the secretaries were released on one Friday. Two weeks later, calls began to come in from the sales organization trying to understand why their new contracts had not been approved and their customers were waiting for deliveries. After several frantic days of investigation the organization realized that the credit check procedure had been initiated and managed by one of the sales department's secretaries who had been let go. The secretary was immediately called and agreed to work for the company on a consulting basis for four times her previous salary.

operation and not just a future potential operation, that is needed to make much more targeted cuts and improve the chances that they will adhere to the first rule of change, taken from the Hippocratic Oath: "First, do no harm."

ASSUMPTION 5.3
WHEN THERE IS A RIF, THE APPROPRIATE PEOPLE WILL BE CUT.

Reductions in force, or RIFs, are often conducted on the assumption that the manager of an area will cut the right people. This is generally considered a positive action since, in theory, the unproductive will be released. And, where this is true, the organization does in fact benefit. But as often as not, either the cuts must go too deep or the manager just eliminates staff based on personal bias instead of the real value of people to the company. The result is that good people are released with the nonperformers.

While these cuts have often succeeded in meeting short-term financial goals, they have driven many companies to their knees. An example of the failure of this approach is the IBM cutbacks of several years ago. Over 40,000 people were released in massive reductions. The company was going to run lean and mean. It did— almost. IBM found they couldn't run quite as lean and mean as they thought. The company hired a great many people back as consultants. Also, because many senior technical people were released, the ability of IBM to continue to be an innovator in advanced technologies is now in question. But, while time will tell whether IBM will remain an innovator, there is no question as to the lack of success of the staff reduction.

In contrast, Empire Blue Cross/ Blue Shield's National Claims Processing group believed that their workforce could basically be divided into knowledge workers and unskilled staff. The knowledge workers were highly trained insurance and claims specialists. In fact, they believed that it took almost three years to create a senior claims adjudicator. In the belief that these people were really an investment in quality and success, the vice president of the area decided that staff cuts would be limited to unskilled workers. The skilled group remained intact, and allowed National Claims to be ready for an expansion that is now occurring. While this approach did not reduce costs as much as an across-the-board cut would have, it has been much more effective for the long-term viability of the operation.

The fact is that reductions in staff that are not accompanied by reductions in the work, reductions in production levels, or reductions in levels of specific skill requirements usually do not work. The real value of employees is in their skills. Few companies have a detailed, central index of what skills are needed throughout the company, where a given skill is used, or the real value of that skill. Most companies rely instead upon management by position descriptions, which usually fail to address real skills and are generally out of touch with the real work that is being done. This has made a skill-based assessment a tough order. It has also made any focused reduction almost impossible.

As a result, few people have been protected against reductions and many companies have released the wrong people. Both their business operations and their abilities to compete have suffered. There is also a negative impact on the workers who remain: they are less motivated to do good work and to learn new skills because they have seen that neither protects them from being RIF'd.

Reductions in force do make a company lean and mean. They create big holes, ill will, and unexpected future expenses. If there is another way, just don't do RIFs.

ASSUMPTION 5.4
STAFF ARE ADEQUATE, IN BOTH NUMBERS AND SKILL, BUT THEY ARE NOT USED EFFECTIVELY.

Although few managers can do more than provide one or two specific examples, most believe that many of the people in the company are not being used effectively. This position is supported by many staff members who concur and are not shy about telling anyone who will listen that they can do much more than they are allowed to do.

In fact, few companies are really able to determine how well their workforces are being used. Therefore the assumption that staff are used badly is both valid and invalid in almost every company. Some employees are overutilized and some are not being used effectively; some can contribute much more and would welcome the chance to do so. Challenging this assumption provides answers that may yield surprising results: increased effectiveness, increased productivity, improved quality, and substantial improvements in morale.

Ineffective use of employees can become a significant problem when management becomes complacent. As attention is shifted away from individual staff contributions, many assignments are made based on expediency: who is immediately available?

As expediency becomes the prevailing criterion in personnel assignment, many managers become burdened with short-term fire fighting. It is then easy for them to lose sight of how staff are being assigned to an even greater extent, so that the abilities of many staff members can easily be underutilized. This has often been a key driver in staff turnover as the better people feel frustrated and have a low sense of self-worth.

Because many managers believe that their biggest problem is retaining good people, this assumption can cause an aggravation that could be avoided. Without a clear understanding of operational needs and opportunities along with a detailed and current skills inventory for the knowledge workers and those being trained to become knowledge workers, the proper alignment of staff with jobs is difficult. Many managers believe this is one of their primary responsibilities.

At Elkay, Inc., a manufacturing company headquartered in Oak Brook, Illinois, a Chicago suburb, the Information Technology group is run on the principle that staff growth is a key management responsibility. They consider skills and skill enhancement in most of their assignments. This I/T group has implemented some simple automated aids and some uniform methods for assignment of technical staff to all of its projects. As a result, staff are better utilized for each current project, and the professional growth of every staff member becomes an asset for the company, to be realized in the future.

In many respects this type of consideration is an age-old concern of consulting firms. Staff growth equates to flexibility in obtaining work. The more skilled people are, the higher their rates and the more value they offer to the firm and the client. The same concept has often been found in progressive information systems groups. Unfortunately, this is rarely the case in operational areas. Here training is typically provided by internal trainers, and the information that is taught is often known by the operations managers to be inaccurate and out of date. This situation is the reverse side of the underutilization problem. Here assignments are made based on assumed skills that are not adequate. In these cases the company, the employees, and the products suffer.

The proper evaluation of staff skills and abilities is critical in any operation. But when the utilization assumptions are not challenged, errors on both sides of the assignment issue are inevitable.

ASSUMPTION 5.5
STAFF NEED ONLY MINIMAL INFRASTRUCTURE AND FACILITY SUPPORT.

The good news is that recent studies have indicated that the overall impression of the workforce is that their working conditions are adequate and that they are well supported as employees. While we are certain this is true for many companies, it is clearly not true for all. In many companies staff members are asked to work harder to overcome equipment problems, space problems, and environment problems.

Every company is faced with the growing problems of providing adequate computer support for its staff. As PC use proliferates in companies, the need for more capable machines creates a continuing requirement for new equipment and new software, both costing a lot of money. Not many companies have been able to keep up with the need and many people are asked to make do with older, less capable equipment.

In some cases, this closes many people off from the systems they need and creates confusion and "work-around" activity. Not only is a lot of time lost, but untold errors are introduced into management reports as reports are rekeyed, rearranged, and reedited. In addition to computers, other equipment, including telephones, is at a premium in some operations. In one company that relies heavily on customer interaction, we saw up to fifteen people sharing one telephone. In this same company we saw the same numbers of staff using a single imaging workstation to look up information. This caused backlogs and required an ineffective approach to grouping work.

Space is also at a premium in most companies, which is surprising considering the trend to reductions in force. Office and meeting space is almost nonexistent in many companies. Meetings must be scheduled far in advance and groups working on special projects have trouble finding places to meet. This is a key reason that decisions and coordination take an inordinate amount of time and few projects move at the pace needed to allow the company to compete.

When an operation is forced to work around more than one of these limiting factors, it becomes extremely inefficient. Work is slow and labor-intensive. To conserve support costs, the company pays higher payroll expenses, because more people are needed. The real problem is that the ability of the company to compete is reduced by increased product costs and unnecessary delays.

For example, in a large insurance company, claims processors were not provided with the computer terminals they needed to track and process claims properly. The result was a time-consuming manual process that cost the company weeks of processing time. When an error was encountered, the weeks turned into months.

This assumption is generally not challenged because challenging it requires funding. At a time when budgets are being cut and holding costs is critical, most managers look at attempts to obtain additional technology, space, or environmental niceties as little more than a waste of time. And with all the work that must be done, few managers want to waste any time.

ASSUMPTION 5.6
THE ORGANIZATION NEEDS TO BE FLATTENED; THE SPAN OF CONTROL OF A MANAGER SHOULD BE 20 OR MORE PEOPLE.

Moving to a flatter, less hierarchical organization has been touted as the way to improve everything from quality to productivity. While reports on the success of moves to flatten structures are mixed, the assumption that this move is right for every business should be challenged.

The real problem is not with the concept, but with the way many companies have implemented it. When the "just get rid of middle or line management" approach is used, the majority of these managers are simply eliminated overnight. This creates a void. The assumption that the managers who are left will understand the work at the lower levels or in other organizations that they are now responsible for just has no basis. Managers do not always know how work is being done one level, let alone two levels, below them. Although many disagree with this statement, it can easily be tested by asking any manager to randomly pick a person working in the manager's unit and try to do that person's work. Few managers will succeed.

When the middle layer of management is eliminated, the reality is that the more detailed knowledge of how the operation really works is lost. When the upper layer of managers now must take over a wider span of direct control, this lack of knowledge often causes problems. Not only do managers not know how the details work, they cannot expect much assistance from the staff. These people are not used to thinking from the perspective of their immediate supervisor, let alone a level or two above their old manager. The disconnection in perspective, understanding, and control is a serious problem in many companies. Communication also often breaks down as a level of translation in both directions, management to staff and staff to management, is removed.

Another key problem with the flattening of organizations is an inability to perform needed management and financial studies. For example, cost benefit analysis studies, requirements definition, project management and reporting, and problem analysis skills are often impaired or eliminated when middle and line managers are cut. In some cases, the ability of the organization to comply with such financial requirements as request-for-proposal creation, multivendor consideration, and proposal evaluation is virtually impossible. These skills, which are a normal part of the middle and line managers'jobs, do not exist in the lower levels of staff who are left.

The role of the manager often also changes in a flattened structure. Managers become reviewers and they often do not have the time to do a good job of planning or taking care of staff problems. In these cases management becomes increasingly depersonalized—there is just not enough time to establish a close relationship with 20 or 30 people. Staff often become demoralized when this occurs.

While some flattening can often be desirable, it is clear that severe flattening is often not the right answer. When it is proposed, it should be challenged and forced to prove its merits.

ASSUMPTION 5.7
THE COMPANY IS NOT LEAN. THERE MUST BE MANY
PLACES WHERE STAFFING CAN BE REDUCED.

As business entered the 1990s, the battle cry of the finance department was "We are fat! We need to cut costs!" Neither finance nor human resources (HR) has been very accurate in locating where the supposed fat was or how much of it there really was. With no precise metrics to start with, many managers unquestioningly accepted the estimates of Michael Hammer (coauthor of *Reengineering the Corporation*) who wrote that all companies could cut about 40 percent. Hence the goal of cost reduction efforts often became 40 percent without any specific information to substantiate that target. In fact, while some of these efforts exceeded the 40 percent goal, many more failed. Significant cost reductions were usually made, but the efforts were frequently considered failures because they did not hit their targets.

In almost all industries, it is true that there is some fat. But the fat is often very widely dispersed. Employees rarely just waste time (now that businesses have learned to outlaw computer games). There are few apparent abuses in staffing levels when viewed from this perspective. The fat comes in through wasted work. Most processes have tremendous amounts of non-value-added work. Redundancies are rampant and busywork is not hard to find. This is where the fat is. It is found in small percentages of many people's time. This is also the fallacy of shotgun mass reductions in force. Eliminating a person eliminates available effort, not work. The same amount of work must still be done. The issue is how to find out what can be cut and how to reduce the amount of work along with staff reductions. No one has succeeded in reducing expenses by starting only with the feeling that there must be fat in the operation.

Staff reductions based on poor financial projections have often targeted this perceived fat. But because no one knew where any wasted person-power was to be found, this sort of cutback has usually caused more harm than good (assuming that the company would not have gone out of business unless staff-related dollars were cut as soon as possible).

The "we are fat" assumption must obviously be challenged. It must be clearly identified as a hidden assumption and either proven valid or discarded. The impact of corporate liposuction cannot be taken for granted as a benefit. A favorable outcome is not assured. Many companies have found, sadly, that the savings gained are more than offset by the expense of adjusting to the loss in productivity, continuity, and knowledge.

A large east coast insurance company cut costs in 1992 by eliminating information technology staff. Senior managers were very certain that there were more people than necessary in that area, and they insisted on a large cutback. The CIO chose the technical writers as part of the fat-trimming and eliminated the entire group. Programmers were considered to be of more value. The result was that the documentation for their main computer system was simply not updated. Over the past four years literally hundreds of changes have been made to improve the system and to correct problems. The documentation was not modified. Today, no one knows exactly how the system works. Changes are based on guesswork as the programmers try to track impact through the actual program code. As a result, the ripple effect of changes causes significant problems and the time needed to evaluate, estimate, and make changes is much greater than it would have been if the technical writers had not been eliminated. The operational areas are suffering, the information technology group is suffering, and the customers are suffering.

ASSUMPTION 5.8
BECOMING MORE EFFICIENT MEANS CUTTING STAFF.

This is probably one of greatest fallacies in modern business. Becoming more efficient has little to do with cutting staff. Cutting staff is clearly a bottom-line issue. Efficiency is clearly an operational issue. The two cross paths only when staff cuts are preceded by process improvement efforts. Many businesses cut staff in the incorrect belief that the people who are left will automatically become more efficient—after all, everyone knows that all companies are overstaffed and fat (see Assumption 5.7).

The problem is that many companies have acted based on this assumption, but efficiency improvement has not been achieved. What have been achieved are cost reductions that are often temporary. The price for these cost savings is increased stress, anxiety, frustration, disenfranchisement, and anger.

In most cases, becoming more efficient means reducing the amount of work that must be done. In other cases, efficiency relates to the amount of work that can be done by a person in a given time. Generally, improvement in the amount of work that can be done is related to improved computer or other technologies. The use of technology provides a type of work reduction by moving the work from a person to a machine. In either case, work is reduced. The number people who are needed to handle a given volume of work can thus be reduced. But efficiency is gained first, and then staff is adjusted based on a reduced work volume.

At a large Midwest food producer, management decided to cut clerical staff in the engineering group. This was done and engineering was reorganized and centralized. Politics were ignored in this process. The result was that the relocated engineers were looked at as outsiders and there was no sense of unity or group loyalty. Every person stood alone. The strain was increased further as the engineers had to absorb the clerical work—no improvements in process had been made, so the volume of clerical work did not change. The result was an unhappy staff that had to spend a significant part of their time on low-level work. When schedules began to slip and vendors began to experience delays in payments while Accounts Payable waited for the engineers to approve the work and equipment installation, management recognized its mistake.

ASSUMPTION 5.9
WE CANNOT FIND OR KEEP GOOD PEOPLE.

This assumption appears to recognize the value of people to a company, which is good. But accepting it also means that the company considers its existing staff less than capable, and sees the remedy as a matter of hiring different people. Managers who hold this assumption really evaluate their staff as lacking capability. The basic difference of opinion is that some managers feel a wide range of people can do most work if they are trained and motivated properly, while other managers disagree. It is a difficult difference to resolve and, therefore, this is a difficult assumption to challenge.

The controversy begins at the top. In a recent IBM study, CEOs reported that their single most important problem was their inability to attract and keep good staff. While this is not a new issue, the problem seems to be growing worse, even while jobs are harder to find and corporate downsizing is common.

Staff are a company's most basic asset. From a financial perspective, money, bricks, and mortar are all that seem to be important; but the ability of a company to remain in business is related more directly to people and how they perform. It is the human resources that decide what business the company will be in and what products will be made. People build, manufacture, or supply the service or product; and people market and support the administration of the operation. In highly successful companies, people are always recognized as the key to maintaining a competitive edge.

The question is: in order to improve, should the company take steps to get better people, or should the current staff be given more opportunity to become increasingly competent? It is obviously safest to do both. Unfortunately, neither approach is easy.

To obtain and retain good people, effective recruiting is obviously essential. However, there are other factors as well. One of these factors, a key aspect of recruitment, retention, and staff improvement, is that the company commit to supporting the staff. Management's attitude toward support determines the corporate culture, the work environment, and obviously the staff's motivation. Another factor is the workplace itself. When management's attitude and the workplace are not first-rate, the company is left with no choice but to settle for mediocre staff.

In the early 1990s, a project was initiated to reengineer the information services operation and several processes at a Fortune 500 publishing company. The company was located in a suburb of Chicago that was difficult to get to and the physical environment left much to be desired. To provide internal support for the reengineering project, the company needed to hire several people with specialized technology skills. The search was carried on for months with little real progress. Several people were brought on board during this time, but they were seldom the best that were interviewed. Few people wanted to work in the poor conditions that were provided and few people wanted to work for the managers they spoke to. The quality of the support that was available to the company was marginal. The ability of the company to move to more current technologies that were approved and planned was so minimal that the effort was a very high risk. The result was a marginal capability that cost the same as a very flexible, high-quality support service. As a result, several strategic efforts were canceled and market share was lost. Also, as failure became apparent, many of the best people left. This moved the company further toward mediocre support and performance.

ASSUMPTION 5.10
WE CANNOT TRUST OUR STAFF. THEY ARE LAZY, THEY WILL CHEAT, AND THEY WILL STEAL ANYTHING THEY CAN.

Unfortunately, this assumption is held by many managers in many companies. It is never true, but often staff will live up (or down) to management's expectations. If managers believe in their staff and the staff understand the confidence that has been placed in them, they generally rise to most requirements. We have seen that when management and staff have a good relationship, most people want to do a good job. We also believe that most people want to take pride in their work. Where this is not happening, we often find a hostile management group that views its relationship with staff as adversarial. These managers generally have very low expectations, and the staff fulfill them.

The quality of the workforce is also an important factor in setting expectations. If the workforce is comprised of people with bad attitudes or poor work ethics, the stage is set for confrontation. This generally is a ripe environment for unions and union actions.

In most cases, we have found that in companies where people have a high personal regard for management and trust in the company, they consistently give additional time and effort. They are willing to go the extra mile.

A contributor to the problem and one of the biggest reasons that process improvement efforts fail in many operations is the compensation system. These systems often encourage cheating, sloth, and lying. They make it personally profitable for managers and staff to operate in their own best interests. Few compensation packages that we see are directed toward achievements that are to the advantage of the company.

Companies that motivate their people find this assumption to be false. The important difference is the ability to understand how each person contributes and leverage this understanding into a belief that personal success is only achieved through corporate success.

In one operation, Human Resources' policy stated that nonexempt staff could only be paid an hourly rate. Many of these people met their daily production quotas by 10 a.m. and virtually did nothing for the rest of the day. They had met their quotas. As far as HR was concerned, they deserved adequate performance ratings. As far as the people were concerned, they were happy to do nothing for the remainder of the day and get paid for it. The incentive program was obviously flawed. It was recommended that the compensation approach be moved to a base salary that was low, with incentives being provided by a per-piece pay addition. When it was tried in a test, production tripled. However, HR would not relent and the compensation program was not changed. The culture and the lack of flexibility within the company and the HR group did not allow improvement.

ASSUMPTION 5.11
THERE ARE REALLY NO SELF-MOTIVATED, ETHICAL EMPLOYEES. THEY ARE ALL JUST OUT FOR THEMSELVES.

Managers, knowledge workers, and skilled and unskilled workers have been thought to follow different work ethics for the past several hundred years. Today, much of that belief is changing.

The attitude of people regarding their loyalty and the amount of sacrifice they will make for a company is generally becoming consistent among all levels of management and staff in larger companies. Few people in any company believe the top managers care all that much about the long-term viability of the company. Incentive packages in many companies simply preclude a long-term perspective.

This assumption is less frequently valid among professional and technical personnel. In technical areas, exempt employees often have a very different attitude than lower-level workers. For example, information services staff typically put in much more than the time officially required by the company. They carry beepers and are called at all hours of the day and night. When a system has a problem, they are called in to fix it, no matter what the time of day. Among professional staff, accountants and internal audit staff often put in long hours, due to the amounts of detailed work they do and the deadlines they have to meet.

However, in cases where loyalty and trust have been sacrificed, this assumption is often valid. This is typical in the nonexempt employee ranks. Here the age-old struggle often exists: management vs. labor. Many managers believe this is the natural state—a belief we disagree with. The key is building relationship and trust. To move forward in creating a learning, highly productive organization, this assumption must be challenged.

ASSUMPTION 5.12
EMPLOYEES SHOULD BE GLAD THEY HAVE JOBS, AND SHOULD THEREFORE BE LOYAL TO THE COMPANY.

This assumption is clearly based on the belief that people will feel grateful for their jobs. Gratitude is an uncertain element at best. Loyalty cannot be based on gratitude. People are simply not grateful for anything for very long. The old question, "What have you done for me lately?" can be applied to this assumption to put the concept of loyalty in perspective. Also, the broken trust of downsizing is forcing a fairly short-term perspective on the part of many managers and staff members. The belief that if they were loyal and hard-working they would be taken care of by the company has been crushed.

In recent years, the response of many managers to the lack of loyalty in most companies has been that the disloyal persons should be "glad they have jobs." True enough, but again gratitude does not produce loyalty. The primary driver of loyalty seems to be trust. Where there is trust in the management group, there is loyalty. Unfortunately, trust cannot be gained through threats, pay increases (bribes), or promises. Trust requires a commitment to fairness and dedication to the staff—and not just to the bottom line.

Two people moved from Chicago to New Mexico in the summer of 1996. The husband had recently been RIFed, a victim of a large downsizing at a Chicago-area company that makes lawn mowers. His story was fairly common. He had worked for the company for 23 years, most of his career. To cut costs, management had eliminated the number of people needed to provide the required dollar savings. His bitterness was obvious. He felt cheated and abused. The result was that he felt he would never trust a company again. He would put in his time and work well enough to get by, but he would never again be loyal. Furthermore, he would spread the word about his former employer to anyone who would listen. He had become the company's worst enemy.

His wife, on the other hand, loved her company, Enterprise Car Rental. She, in fact, did her best to convince anyone she had a few minutes conversation with that they should switch from their customary rental car company to Enterprise. She was a great sales representative, going on and on about how good Enterprise was. There was no question about her loyalty. In fact, she had no intention of leaving Enterprise and had already obtained approval for a transfer to a local rental office in New Mexico. No one bought her loyalty. No one threatened it into her. She trusted the company and believed that it would never do what the lawn mower manufacturer did to her husband.

Loyalty does not have to be won by a business. It is there for the business to appreciate or to destroy. Too often the latter course is chosen.

ASSUMPTION 5.13
ALL OF OUR MANAGERS CARE FOR THEIR PEOPLE.

Naive, but this assumption is often stated or implied whenever personnel issues are brought up. It is firmly embedded in most company cultures. Each company has a unique group of cultures that must be understood if any cross-organizational effort is to succeed. In analyzing the cultures of a company, identifying the attitudes of managers toward one another and toward their staff is critical. Managers are supposed to take care of their employees, so the assumption is made that they do. It is usually a good idea to challenge it: many managers have no concern for their people.

Where there is genuine concern for the staff, the company generally enjoys the benefits gained from high staff morale. They also often have loyal staff. Here is an example of one company that succeeds in taking care of its employees and reaps the benefits of this practice.

In a West Coast software company, a progressive, people-oriented firm, management has stated that "having fun" is so important that it is part of the formal mission statement. They live up to it. The company has about 200 employees, and a caring culture permeates the entire organization. On the first snow day of the year, everyone leaves early to go skiing. On the day the salmon start running, everyone goes fishing. Nice environment. But the staff also understand schedules and mutual support. The employees reciprocate: it is common for staff members to work long hours without threats or incentives. They do what is needed to get the job done. The company is very successful. The good treatment that they offer their employees works well for them.

This company's specific policies are not for everyone. They would not work in a larger company.

In most companies, managers truly care for the people directly reporting to them. While this is not universal and is obviously a broad generalization, many managers have a genuine concern for many of their staff. Many, but not all. That's human nature and that's why there are fairness laws—to make certain managers' likes and dislikes are kept in check. The problem is that caring and fairness cannot be assumed. Both rely on the temperaments of individual managers and their "management styles." Even caring managers are affected by outside factors that can override their concern. Among the most common of these factors is the pressure to get the job done. Most managers believe that if they do not succeed in even ridiculous requests, their bosses will "find someone who can succeed." They react to these pressures by passing them on to their employees.

In summary, this assumption reflects the underlying character of management. Challenging the assumption, the company's entire management climate must be reviewed.

ASSUMPTION 5.14
ALL EXEMPT EMPLOYEES SHOULD BE WILLING TO GIVE WHATEVER TIME IS NEEDED.

This assumption was valid for many years, but now it is being questioned and in some cases it does not reflect the attitudes of lower-level exempts. Therefore, it should now be questioned, rather than relied upon.

Most managers are faced with the problem of doing more with fewer people. As the pressures build to produce, the requirement to give more time and work harder often increases.

In two Chicago grocery chains, the meat cutters, who were union workers, were required to work an extra ten hours a week, without pay. This was an unofficial rule that was enforced. Any meat cutter who objected was fired. The union turned its head. The workers gave the extra time because they had no choice. As a result, the work ethic was poor and morale was worse. Customer service was not considered to be important and the workers did not put forth their best efforts. In reality, the company won a labor battle but lost the war. They did get the time but, with generally low productivity, they lost during every hour of the workday.

Here is another case, in which teachers were forced to put forth more and more effort, a little at a time, until the school system almost collapsed.

A school system in a Chicago area suburb used its principals to encourage teachers to serve on committees. While this worked well for some time, some principals became overeager and forced teachers to participate on many committees—and spend a considerable amount of personal time in preparation and meetings. For some months the teachers agreed and there was no problem. However, the principals began to expect sacrifices as a matter of course. They often failed to recognize the teachers' individual contributions and failed to give back time when the teachers needed it. The situation clearly became too one-sided. Today, the relationships have become hostile. Morale is low and stubbornness is setting in on both sides. The principals threaten the teachers and the teachers cite the union contract. The teachers want to provide the highest quality education they can. The school district wants the same thing. The principals have lost perspective, and rely on the assumption that the teachers should do anything they are asked to do. A motivated teaching staff has become frustrated and an administration has stopped caring.

The issue is not whether people will give extra effort or time; both can be forced. The only real question is, "Is it worthwhile?" Clearly in the cases we have seen, the overall results were not positive. The immediate solutions did get the work done, but overall productivity and the relationship between the company and the staff suffered.

ASSUMPTION 5.15
ANYONE CAN BE REPLACED.

A common belief among many managers is that everyone can be replaced, with the possible exception of themselves. To be fair to the many managers who really believe this assumption, some actually do place themselves in the expendable category. This assumption is at the base of virtually every reduction in force and most financially-driven downsizings.

But is it really valid? Over the years, two factors have proven it incorrect. First, business people work very hard to make themselves indispensable, and many have succeeded. Second, few companies have made the effort to document how the business really works and who does what, when they do it, and how they do it. This understanding is a primary driver behind the formalization of disaster recovery programs.

So, what might happen if you lost a given person? Clearly, in many cases, disaster will strike. For example, among the most critical staff members are those in the information technology departments. Although most managers do not believe that their computer support is adequate, most cringe at the thought of losing the one or two people who know how to fix their systems and keep them running. And the same is true for any critical part of the company.

In some cases the lack of truth in this assumption results in the company literally being held hostage by an employee. These people become highly paid and arrogant. They threaten to leave and they refuse to document anything. They force increasing reliance and they enjoy a great deal of power within their own limited spheres of influence.

Of course, at times the reliance on a person can go unnoticed. This is the most dangerous case because there is no way to circumvent the situation. It is just a hidden land mine that can get you at any time. If the company is lucky, the explosion will occur when the person is still available to assist in correcting the problems that result from their leaving. Sometimes, as in this example, the company is not lucky.

Clearly, operations change constantly. People adjust to the changing needs through creativity—they find a way to get the job done. But most of these changes go unnoticed by management. A large manufacturer cut back clerical staff across the company. Suddenly, a critical report that the CEO used to monitor activity was unavailable. The CEO was incensed. Everyone began to scramble, but the report could not be reproduced. After several days of investigation and the creation of a workflow model, the source of the report was uncovered. The CEO's assistant had obtained the numbers from a secretary in another area, not from a computer report. The secretary, who had been let go, had been calling several other secretaries to obtain specific numbers. In one situation, the secretary who compiled the report had called a friend in the plant to get the base numbers. The trail that the numbers in the lost report had taken was long and anything but straightforward. Several of the secretaries who had been involved were let go, and the ability to produce the report had unknowingly been cut with them. The cost of finding the data and reestablishing the report was higher than the savings from cutting the secretaries from the payroll.

CHALLENGING HUMAN RESOURCES ASSUMPTIONS

Almost every business wants to improve its human resources. Small gains in the competence of a company's employees will result in many benefits. People are a company's greatest asset. However, people are also the most complex aspect of business, so making improvements is not easy.

Because this book emphasizes the assumptions we have found are most often taken for granted, the way to begin making improvements is by changing awareness and attitudes. Without these changes, everything else will provide only short-term results. Admittedly, attitudes are the most resistant to change.

FIRST, IMPROVE INDIVIDUAL ATTITUDES

There are managers with destructive attitudes in positions of responsibility in many companies. Where their influence is felt, the operation is ineffective. Managers in positions of responsibility tend to build walls around themselves and isolate their operations from the corporate world. They do not return phone calls or answer their E-mail. They are always too busy to do anything and they are always in some meeting or other discussing obscure but important issues. The employees working in these areas tend to follow their manager's example and any cooperation with other operational units is minimal. Trust is nonexistent in these operations and their people, and frustration levels are high.

In addition to the isolationist manager, "lip service" managers are also a real impediment to moving forward. These people say what they think others want to hear and then develop convenient amnesia. Their commitments are never met and their position on any issue is both unclear and constantly shifting. While excuses are given for nothing getting done, the ultimate result is a total lack of progress: nothing improves. Lip service managers are easy to find. The visible evidence is an inordinate amount of rhetoric with no real improvement and constant complaints about the amount of work that must be done with too few staff. A lot of work seems to be taking place, according to the manger, but nothing is really happening.

THE DIFFERING GOALS OF INDIVIDUALS AND THE COMPANY: STRATEGIC ALIGNMENT

One of the most damaging fallacies in business is the assumption that the goals of the company are the goals of all managers and staff members. First, few staff members even know that there are corporate goals (other than slogans) in most companies. Fewer still know what the goals are. Almost no working-level employees know how the corporate goals affect them, or how they can help to attain them. This lack of knowledge is one of the chief causes of the general misalignment so common in business. This problem exists even in companies that have invested in formal, multimillion-dollar strategic plans. Working-level managers and staff members are simply not in tune with corporate planning in most companies.

This situation is very difficult to remedy, but it can be done if the company is willing to put forth the effort. The alignment of goals begins with the alignment of planning in the company, from the CEO to the working levels. It entails stripping out individual and departmental interpretations of the company's plans, and any extraneous personal objectives. It continues by engaging the staff in accomplishing all of the plan's specific goals. Everyone then knows how they will personally contribute and why their work is important.

This alignment is a key step in the battle against corporate politics and, if even partially successful, will significantly strengthen a company.

CORPORATE CULTURE AND COMPANY POLITICS

Culture is made up of the attitudes and approaches to business of the people within a company. It is the foundation for the institution of corporate politics. While there is nothing new in identifying the existence of politics, there is something very different about formally recognizing their existence and declaring war. Politics arise where the goals of the individual and the company diverge. Culture includes a business' hidden assumptions.

Unlike politics, culture has its good side. Culture provides some consistency to activities that are not formally controlled. Culture gives a sense of security to the employees. Indeed, the negative side of culture is only greatly troublesome when it is an obstacle to change. Challenging assumptions related to politics is risky, but important. Given the risk, however, they can only be challenged at high levels in most companies. To a lesser degree, individual managers can successfully challenge the politics below them in their operations. This will have a lesser impact, but it is still important to win small victories.

Both culture and politics can best be challenged by examining hidden assumptions, especially those related to general management, human resources, and planning.

WHEN EMPOWERMENT DOES NOT EMPOWER

Anyone who has seen much of business believes in empowerment. It is almost a given: everyone in every business needs the authority to do a job as effectively as it can be done. However, specific attempts to empower individuals and groups have had only mixed success. While the reasons are many and varied, one of the chief empowerment problems is the existence of hidden assumptions, specifically those in this chapter related to human resources. Empowerment cannot occur where there is no trust and where staff and management are at odds. Consider the following: a company has just downsized, maybe for the third or fourth time. The ranks are getting thin. Good workers have been fired; no one knows who will be next. Now management says, "Everything is fine now. We believe in those who are left and we want to give them more authority." However, trust in management no longer exists. Employees will still be afraid of making wrong decisions, more so than ever before. They are afraid that wrong decisions will be used against them in the next round of downsizing. And, in most companies, staff members believe there will always be more downsizing. So many "empowered" people play it safe. They make no decisions and do nothing that would be considered to be progressive or controversial. This is not real empowerment.

JUST DON'T RELY ON MASS LAYOFFS

While mass layoffs usually boost stock prices temporarily, they do nothing to help the company in the longer term. Whenever there is a choice among cost improvements, staff reduction should be last on the list. Of course, there are situations where mass layoffs are needed. When a company changes strategic direction or eliminates a line of business, layoffs are clearly appropriate, but they are never appropriate as financially expedient temporary measures. It just costs the company too much in terms of flexibility, knowledge, skills, loyalty, and, consequently, money.

THE CONFLICT BETWEEN THE HUMAN RESOURCES GROUP AND OPERATIONS

A war is going on between operations and the Human Resources department. This is unfortunate, and it must be remedied. The conflict at first glance seems unavoidable. The goals of the two areas are in opposition. HR must act as if trained monkeys or robots could do every job but the CEO's (they usually do not imply that sort of thing about the CEO). Operations must get the best people they can in order to succeed. This conflict is meant to provide a check and balance. The philosophy is not so much outdated as it is invalid to begin with.

Most senior managers admit that their greatest problem, after change management, is finding and retaining good people. Any situation that impairs the ability of the company to get the staff it needs cannot be tolerated. Senior management should take an operational view of this issue. It is important that the operational areas be organized, designed, and staffed to succeed.

Where necessary, consider overhauling the HR function. The principal concern of HR should not be to protect the company against its staff and lawsuits. Nor should HR be in place to support an HR bureaucracy. The primary function of HR must be to improve the productivity of the business through training, counseling, and assisting in organization development.

Many HR functions are viewed as roadblocks to progress by operational managers. In their quest to protect the business, they make most personnel actions almost impossible. This must be changed. HR must become a partner to the operational managers. Its function should expand far beyond the attainment of staff. The future HR function should break down the barriers that currently exist in most companies between them and the operational areas. The real value of HR lies in its ability to develop the staff's skills and capabilities as the business changes. They should also be the guardians of morale, stress, and attitude. This, of course, requires a very different HR function than currently exists in most companies.

PEOPLE AS ASSETS?

People are the basic asset of every company. Knowledge and skills are the real value of people. Train, train, train. Test skills and knowledge every day: it will provide spice to the job. The financial people are wrong to think of people as liabilities and just base numbers on a spreadsheet. People are the lifeblood of the company. Bricks and mortar are transient in the long run. The creativity, skills, and knowledge of the staff are the only real living part of a company.

CHALLENGING THE HUMAN SIDE OF ENTERPRISE

The first step in challenging assumptions related to the invaluable human resource is to determine what the company really wants from the staff. Design the company not just from the organization standpoint. Add the process view, the quality view, skills and competencies and environmental considerations—the situation in which a person works (space, communications, equipment, the facility, etc.). Align all operational units and the people within them. The goal of each worker, and manager, should be a specific part of the goal of the company. Redefine the jobs of the staff and the effectiveness of the operation based on metrics and feedback from staff, managers, and customers. See *Out of the Crisis*, MIT Cases, 1982, by W. Edwards Deming.

Staff should be used and evaluated more creatively. Which lasts longer—the position or the person? If the company focuses on people rather than the mythical ideal of the position, HR can develop staff along the lines of their greatest talents and aptitudes. This not only creates knowledge workers as people learn more about different areas of the company, it also promotes the most effective use and growth of staff resources.

How can one do this? The answer lies in organizing the business to the extent possible as a series or collection of small, self-motivated teams. This is the organizational format favored by Bill Gates of Microsoft Corp. Rigid hierarchical structures do not lend themselves to the use of staff as individuals. In reality, a compromise will need to be achieved between the classic vertical structure that is generally used and the horizontal team structure that is effective in a wide range of operational cases. This, of course, begins with the review and questioning of all assumptions related to the structure of the business and the attitudes of the managers and staff.

THE THREE VIEWS OF BUSINESS PLANNING

A BUSINESS, LIKE A ROWBOAT, WILL GO
IN CIRCLES IF THE OARS ARE PULLED IN
OPPOSITE DIRECTIONS.

Every business has many formal and informal plans. Some cover change projects; others apply to daily operational management. Each plan is used as interpreted by individual managers in different areas of the business. The multiplicity of plans, further compounded by individual interpretation, creates different views of success and of how the operation should run. While this circumstance is prevalent in most companies, once it is examined, management will want to move to a common view with one set of goals and metrics.

In addition to the differences among all of the working units of the business, there seem to be three pervasive functional groupings of viewpoints. The executive officer focuses on financial success. The line or operational manager's view of success is based on the criteria set for performance: bonus packages and promotions and (hopefully) the need to get the job done. The technician takes the view that the technology can fix all the business's problems: just give them more technology and a better data model.

While these differences are understandable, they splinter a company's direction when they are not formally reconciled. However, when they are recognized as valid perspectives and used to build a comprehensive model of the operation, significantly greater control and effectiveness can be the result. Experience shows that these groups are often out of alignment with the plan and each other. The opportunity and the challenge is to bring these views together in the planning process.

THE THREE VIEWS OF SUCCESS

SENIOR MANAGEMENT.   These managers have a specific responsibility to do two things: remain in business and make money for the stockholders. These requirements necessitate a focused view of the business and of what factors are important. This view relies on high-level measurement systems that are financial in nature. Global issues such as market share and strategy guide the perception and concerns of this group. When looking at the operation and the technology of the company, these people are interested in performance and cost-related issues. Their main concerns are: is the effort on time and in budget? Will it provide the anticipated return on investment?

OPERATIONS.   Operational managers are mid-level and line managers. The perspective of these people is clearly more related to improving the effectiveness and efficiency of the operation. They are typically interested in project budgets and schedules, but these are secondary to the effect the project will have on their ability to succeed in their daily work. The focus of operational managers is on improvement in quality and efficiency as they are defined in the company's measurement systems.

TECHNOLOGY.   The concern of the technology groups is related to the delivery mechanism of the support they provide. This is the computer, or manufacturing/diagnostic/services technology, the communication networks, and the systems that run on them. The technology perspective is related to project completion, equipment requirements, technology infrastructure, and system schedules. Budget is important, but only in terms of measuring project cost. Operational requirements are important, but are up to the user or customer. The focus is on providing support as defined by the operation, making certain new projects do not interfere with current systems, and providing adequate data distribution capabilities.

DIFFERING VIEWS

Clearly each view is needed and each view is appropriate. When each view is kept separate and a composite of the three views is not considered by all involved groups, a disconnection in focus and in the definition of success occurs. In this environment it is common for one group to consider an effort a success and others to consider it a failure. Ultimately, the view of senior management will win, but in many cases, the other views are equally valid for the company. Strategy setting and planning are seriously hampered by ignoring them. Implementation is also much more difficult in this fractured type of corporate environment.

To promote long-term success, the views of all groups must be brought together and formally used to define evaluation criteria and to define the success of major efforts. Through this sharing of perspectives, the evaluation and project committees can gain a true understanding of the effort and the importance of its goals. For example, in all cases cost is important, but when the objective is strategic, cost may be secondary to the creation of certain capabilities. If the project comes in on time and in budget, but does not provide the best infrastructure for the future, the project may be a failure. If it is over the budget but still on time, and provides the best results possible, it may be a success. The criteria for evaluation will vary. Evaluating success based on perspective and a negotiated definition will undoubtedly be more useful than applying the criterion from any single view.

WHAT IS SUCCESS?

As we have seen, managers have views of success that are strongly influenced by their jobs and the criteria by which they are evaluated. The Hungarians say "Where you sit is where you stand." The influence of a manager's assigned responsibilities extends his view of success; it affects nearly all of her opinions.

Managers' jobs also focus their attention, often to the virtual exclusion of everything outside their purview. The natural result of this isolation of concern is that the company must contend with many differing views of what is important and where the business should go. Individual business units naturally define importance based on their own measurement systems. Personal goals and politics often impact the way anyone looks at success. What is important to one is thus probably not important to another. Trying to layer another level of importance, the corporate level, has typically not resulted in a change in definition, ranking, or concept. Managers still focus on what is important to the success of their business units; that's what they are judged on. This is a key contributing factor in the failure of consensus management and many team efforts. The good of the company does not outweigh the good of the individual. No one will (or ought to) hurt himself for the good of the company.

Success must be defined based on a win–win scenario for the individuals involved and for the company. When this occurs the company will succeed. Again, the trick is to align the objectives so that everyone can find some common ground to define victory.

THE KEY TO SUCCESS

There are no overnight solutions, just hard work that is set up to succeed from the start. However, this is where most projects go wrong. Success must be formally defined in terms of specific goals and measurable results. While this is nothing new, the sound application of this simple principle is seldom followed. The reasons are often valid. For example, measurements are often just not being taken. So, how can one judge success? Typically, the target is just a guess and when questioned, there is no real justification behind the numbers. Also, the goals of most projects are fairly broad and many times there is significant room for interpretation. When undefined interpretation controls a project, it cannot succeed. Win or lose, someone will declare the project's defeat. Usually, no one can prove success absolutely, and human nature sides with the skeptical, so the project will be considered a failure if it cannot be proven to be a success.

The single greatest success factor in projects or any business endeavor is a very clear definition of what is needed and how the work will be judged. If this has not been done properly, the project should be stopped until a formally accepted definition can be worked out. The definition of success should include all three perspectives: senior management's, operational management's, and technology's. When the definition is built from these three perspectives, the project has a chance to succeed. Once that is completed, the other key to success is a strong project manager. While project management tools have recently been touted as the answer to successful projects, we have found that enablement technologies or methodologies are nice, but nothing replaces a comprehensive definition of success or an able project manager.

POOR COMMUNICATION, THE NEMESIS OF HUMAN INTERACTION

The result of these differing viewpoints is a disconnection in communication, concept, importance, and direction. Unsatisfactory communication has always been a key impediment to progress. No company really believes that either their internal or external communication is adequate. It is always a problem. Also, as managers have been forced to be introspective in terms of their view of the company, focusing on their own part of the operation, their concepts of success have often become very narrowly focused. Many managers have taken this introspection to the point that they do not care about any other part of the business. "I have enough to be concerned about here. I really can't worry about their problems."

Where this attitude problem exists, technology will not provide assistance. Mailboxes simply fill up and instead of failing to return phone calls, these managers simply ignore their E-mail: the same old problem dressed in a new suit.

The solution is seldom in improved technology. That is addressing an excuse or symptom, and not the problem. This is more of a corporate culture issue than anything else. Many managers assume that nothing can be done about poor communication because the problem is just too prevalent. Real improvement can be achieved, however, when senior management insists upon interdepartmental communication.

PLANNING ASSUMPTIONS

The following assumptions look at some of the more common beliefs in companies all over the U.S. and Europe. These beliefs do not really change from industry to industry or company to company. They certainly take on different nuances from individual cultures, but the basic concepts are the same in most companies.

ASSUMPTION 6.1
ALL AREAS OF THE BUSINESS SHARE A COMMON VIEW OF WHAT IS ESSENTIAL TO THE BUSINESS.

Senior management must operate as though they believed this pre-cept: there is simply no choice. But most senior managers recog-nize that this is an incorrect assumption. Most businesses operate with both vertical and horizontal organization boundaries or silos. The goals of each silo are unique to that unit. There is just not much cross-silo interaction at any level. At the middle and lower operational levels there is almost no formal and little informal shar-ing of business perspectives.

While most companies today have some form of formal plan-ning, there is generally little formal discussion with lower-level managers or staff about the goals and direction of the company. For the most part, the dissemination of this information is left up to the managers and it is assumed that it will filter down through the or-ganization's hierarchy and reach everyone it should reach. Man-agement in most companies know that unfortunately this is not true. The filtering may happen after a fashion, but the message changes, as in a children's game called telephone. In the game a message starts at one end of the "telephone" line and moves by word of mouth around the room. The players then compare the message at the other end of the line. Almost invariably, the mes-sages at the two ends of the line are very different.

To test this assumption, simply ask people at different levels of the company what the company's goals are and how the goals apply to them personally. The answers may surprise any senior manager. If a large enough cross section of managers and staff are asked these questions, senior management may find the disconnections that are causing this disparity of views, which in turn create diffi-culties in meeting goals.

This disconnection of definition and understanding is in-evitable in bottom-up planning. In several companies, unit plans are submitted separately and rolled into a corporate plan. This bottom-up approach may or may not involve any initial direction from senior management in terms of goals. The approach often has a budget implication, and planning and budgeting in these companies are virtually the same thing. The question is, how can the company move forward in a coordinated manner to accomplish specific goals if these goals do not drive the planning process? If it is assumed that these goals are "just known" or are known because a memo has been passed around with broad goal statements, the questioning process outlined above should be considered and implemented.

At a large hospital in the Chicago area, the planning office relied on a bottom-up planning approach. Every department was responsible for submitting a plan and a budget to support it. The management committee then met to discuss the plans and budgets and let the departments know what was approved. The plans and the budgets were then modified and the operational area had their orders. But, when questioned about corporate plans and objectives, the planning department didn't believe that it was necessary for any of the departments to get together to agree on how they would support one another or the goals of the hospital. There was little direction from senior management to the operational units and there was no horizontal integration of the plans. As a result, the "bottom-up planning effort" turned into a dogfight among the departments of the hospital.

When mid-level and line managers are asked if the company has a plan, many say "Sure," but almost none have a copy of it. When asked if they have actually seen it, most say "No, but my boss has spoken to me about it." When asked how their work supports the company, the typical answer is "I don't really know." When asked what the goals of the company are, many can give very broad general answers, like "improve quality," but almost no one can provide details or a plan as to how they will accomplish the corporate goal in their area. Success criteria are moot in these cases. How can one succeed at something that is not defined or understood?

It is important today for everyone in the company to understand the direction, goals, and problems of the company and how each employee can personally contribute to success. Accomplishing this level of communication requires the creation of a structure that guides planning and expectation definition from the top through all the levels of the company to the lowest staff member. This starts with an honest look at current levels of understanding and asking the question, "Does everyone understand where we are going and what they can do to get us there?"

ASSUMPTION 6.2
EVERYONE WANTS THE PLAN'S OBJECTIVES TO BE MET.

On the surface this seems to go without saying. Everyone wants the company to succeed. But when the corporate objectives conflict with individual objectives, the assumption begins to break down.

First, as stated in Chapter 5, no one will allow corporate objectives to personally hurt them. So, when threat is perceived, the objective will either be changed or ignored. Second, and more importantly, many use the achievement of corporate goals as excuses for personal goals.

> At a company based in Detroit, management wanted to try business process reengineering. They recognized the potential impact on the operation and gave the project a high profile status in the company plan and budget. They then declared their commitment. The high-level mangers put together several teams with the specific charter of cutting staff. When asked about protecting certain people, senior management told the team leaders that no one was to be protected— including themselves. The fate of the project was sealed with that statement. Obviously, the teams found some places to cut staff—where it hurt the most and caused the most disruption. Also, as expected, they did protect themselves and their friends. The project was a distinctly marginal success and the managers blamed the problem on the use of process improvement.

Many managers are evaluated and compensated based on the number of people they manage and the scope of their responsibility. When asked to find ways to cut staff and reduce or eliminate work, the end result is a foregone conclusion. If the company succeeds in the cuts, the managers will personally fail. Without adjustments to the compensation system prior to these types of effort, the managers are motivated to fail. Cuts are often minor and last only a short time. The staffing levels seem almost always to creep back up in these operations.

In many cases, managers privately disagree with the corporate plan or the work it will take to accomplish it. These individuals behave outwardly as if they support the plan, but when progress is reviewed, nothing of any real import has been accomplished. These are the "lip service" managers and staff members. They usually talk a good game, but they have no intention of doing anything except accomplishing their personal goals.

In a third-party review firm in Chicago, corporate management, located in another city, wanted to expand the facility to allow for growth. The location was left up to the local manager. At the time, the facility was located fairly centrally in the western suburban area. The manager used this opportunity to move the facility close to her home in a far northern suburb. The result was a very high turnover of the staff, who were all knowledge workers. The letter of the corporate objective was successfully achieved: they now have a much bigger facility at reasonable rates. The problem was that with the loss of the knowledge workers, the company was severely hurt and its ability to expand was put back several months. Also, the morale of those that stayed was impaired and productivity and trust were sacrificed for personal convenience.

The third dangerous situation is the use of corporate efforts to fuel advancement. Where this is occurring, the manager is often willing to force the effort ahead, even at the expense of other areas and at the expense of the staff on the project. While many senior managers look at this situation as positive ("Just get it done") experience has proven that the cost in disruption can be very high.

All of these situations will appear to be supporting the plan. All will look positive when first reviewed. All are destructive and will only be recognized as destructive when this assumption is questioned and supporting efforts are evaluated in terms of business impact.

ASSUMPTION 6.3
EVERYONE UNDERSTANDS THE COMPANY'S GOALS AND DIRECTION.

When line managers are asked about the company's or their department's strategic or tactical plans one of two answers is generally given. The first is that they don't think the company or their department has a formal plan. The second answer is that there is a plan on paper, but it is really meaningless—no one uses it for anything.

In both situations, the plan is clearly a failure. Unless everyone knows what is expected of them and how their work will allow the company to prosper, it is difficult to obtain the general "buy-in" at all the levels needed for a company to move forward. It is also impossible for the company to move forward in a cohesive manner.

The fact is that in most companies, even those with formal plans created by professional planners, the mid-level and line managers are out of touch with the plans. They are in touch with their budgets, but the bigger picture and the glue that holds the company together for a common purpose is mostly speculation for these people. And if the managers are out of touch, their staffs cannot be expected to have even the foggiest idea of the company's direction or how they fit into it.

The benefits that can be gained by mobilizing the entire workforce around common, clearly defined goals are obvious. They are nothing new and they are the target of most companies. They are also elusive. They cannot be assumed to be the right of any company and they will certainly not be the reward of a company that isolates its lower-level managers and staff from the planning process.

> A former CEO of a large technology company established the corporate goal of cross-functional integration. The first level of management was made very aware of this goal, but did not know how to implement it. Lower-level mangers in the company never even found out about it.

One of the most famous examples of communicating company plans and policy is from Ford Motor Company. When Henry Ford finally relinquished control of the company, the Ford family brought in a new operating head from the FBI. His first act was to arrange that everyone in the company was to have immediate notification of all his acts. This initiative went from the highest levels of management to the lowest levels of the working staff. Even janitors got his memos.

Management also cannot assume that plans will be accurately described to the workers. In most cases there is no description at all. Of course, if management does not accept the need to include as many people as is reasonably possible or inform everyone of the company's goals, problems, direction, and efforts, they need do nothing. Most senior managers, however, do believe this communication is going on or at least that management is doing as much as is possible to distribute this information and solicit comments. For these managers this assumption is important and must be questioned.

In general, few managers really understand what the company must do to succeed. They are often isolated and they clearly understand what they and their people must do to be considered successful. However, they do not really understand the details or specifics of the corporate direction or the real problems facing the company. Commitment begins only with understanding. Taking the right action begins with knowledge. The insulation of the lower-level managers and staff from the corporate-level perspective happens every day. It is often assumed that these people should accept that their orders support the best interest of the company. When the employees do what they are told without question, they are less productive. Creativity and quality improve as people become engaged in working toward a common goal. Again, there is nothing new in these findings. The only real issue is that the assumption—that managers and staff understand how what they are doing supports the company and how their commitment can improve the company—must be challenged and steps must be taken to improve understanding.

ASSUMPTION 6.4
EVERY SENIOR MANAGER IN THE BUSINESS IS WORKING TO DELIVER THE FORMAL BUSINESS PLAN.

We have seen that very few people really know what the goals of the plan are, and logic alone tells us that it is impossible to support something that one is unaware of. However, the problem is often more serious, as some senior managers use the plan as an excuse to further their own personal political interests.

> In a Fortune 500 publishing company, the CIO and the CFO were at war. There was no secret to this war and in fact many employees understood the CIO's position because they were also at war with the CFO and with one another. The opportunity to significantly hurt the CIO came in the form of a CEO mandate to find several million dollars to fund a large strategic planning effort. At the same time, the company was also in the process of pulling its information technology operation out of the middle ages and virtually all systems were to be replaced along with installing the technology infrastructure that was believed to be needed to remain competitive in several of the company's business markets.
>
> In an obvious attack, the CFO brought in a "big six" public accounting firm to evaluate what was going on in the technology area. After all, millions were going to be spent. Of course the report came in that the effort should be suspended pending the outcome of the strategic plan. Why build the wrong technical environment? Funding was cut from technology and diverted to the planning project. The strategic plan took several years. Due to this delay, the technology project was never restarted. The benefits of that project might have made the company successful. Instead, the company's stock has fallen to considerably less than half its former value. Not only has the CFO left, the CIO and the CEO have left as well. In fact, most of the senior officers have been replaced. The systems infrastructure is still not considered by many to be acceptable. But the strategic plan was completed.

In this story, who won? The interests of the company were used as leverage for personal interests. This is a common story. While everyone was working to support the business plan, the means were clearly flawed.

Three factors must be considered in challenging this assumption. First, do people really understand the plan? Second, is the plan right? Finally, do the financial trade-offs and their impact on the plan really make sense?

While it is difficult to identify hidden agendas and personal objectives, the fact is that they not only exist, but they hurt companies every day. This problem is of a sufficient magnitude to merit constant vigilance.

Clearly, enough of the managers in most companies do, in fact, deliver their part of what they perceive the plan to represent. The question is then, why is this an issue? What is the problem? The answer is that to succeed in the future, companies must be prepared to mobilize the workforce in a coordinated manner quickly and move as needed to beat the competition. The nimble company of the future will probably win. But being nimble and responding to competition or opportunity require the constant clarity of vision, purpose, and activity that can only be available when everyone understands the plan, agrees with it, trusts management, and works together to obtain its goals. When this unity is built, the company can change direction almost overnight if necessary, with every chance of success.

A process improvement team at a large western company evaluated the process they were responsible for improving and came up with five significant ideas that would have greatly improved the process according to the metrics that were being used. The manager of the area had a different agenda for himself and the games began. The team began a quest for valid measurements and worked with the floor managers to come up with meaningful ways to measure the improvement and meaningful baseline numbers. At first the metrics showed significant improvements in savings and in cycle time. The manager in charge of the area began to question the metrics and define them according to personal advantage. Although these had no appropriate business foundation, the baseline metrics for the area were changed and the savings calculations were rerun. This process went on for several weeks until a set of metrics was provided that proved that the gains were not important. This clear manipulation of the metrics proved what this manager wanted to prove.

ASSUMPTION 6.5
THE OBJECTIVES OF THE COMPANY ARE THE RIGHT ONES.

Consciously, most executives do not assume that the company is addressing the right objectives. The consideration that they give this issue is, in most cases, just short of agonizing. There are many situations in the planning cycle when perhaps it might be appropriate to return to basics and challenge this assumption, but the idea never surfaces.

The first assumption that should be questioned is: is the company in the right market? Is the market the one that the company should be in next year, or in five years? Is a short-term perspective being followed? Why? If the objective is to sell the company in a year or two, a very different set of goals and objectives will be used from those of a company that wants to remain viable over a long period of time.

Management in many companies simply takes the market and the product direction of the company for granted. A typical statement about market begins with "We are in the x business; that's the business we understand." The question is, are they right?

> The lack of a farsighted understanding of technology and changes in the market allowed Swiss clock companies to give up the electronic digital watch market. They invented the technology and they gave it away. They owned the watch market and they could not understand how it could ever be changed. Texas Instruments and others benefited from the Swiss misunderstanding. These companies now own the greatest percentage of the market.

So, can any management team really be complacent? Can they assume they really understand their market today? Are they properly moving toward tomorrow's market? Clearly, everything about business is changing faster than ever before and keeping up with change is daunting. Unless the objectives of a company are questioned constantly, important technical breakthroughs and buyer patterns will be missed.

To improve the likelihood of being correct about their market, many companies use a laborious process to identify the objectives of the company. The results can be more of a problem than an advantage when they are too broadly or too narrowly defined and when they are used too rigidly. Even if one assumes that the long-range planning process and the market analysis have provided the right direction and the right objectives, the problems of consistency and translation remain.

If the objectives are the right ones, then question whether the high-level objectives have been properly interpreted throughout the company. Are the business units' individual objectives the right ones? Do these lower-level objectives really complement the corporate-level ones? Most often, even if the responses are "yes," and that is not at all guaranteed, a detailed evaluation will likely show a disconnection. Again, the question must be asked: are these really the right objectives? Where this is merely assumed, there exists a real weakness in the ability of the company to change and make the right moves.

ASSUMPTION 6.6
FORMAL PLANS CAN AND WILL BE IMPLEMENTED.

The fallacy of this assumption is clear. Many companies have followed formal plans for years and they are still trying to implement many projects and solve many problems that have been targeted in plan after plan. The fact is that while incorporation into the plan does raise visibility, it does not insure action.

Stating an objective does not mean it can or will be successfully implemented. Anything can be and is included in the plan. Often the objectives are only given cursory attention in larger companies. The real driver in many companies is the budget. The plan certainly supports the budget, but the detail is in the budget, not in the plan. What is the company really committing itself to? And what makes anyone think the goals can or will be completed? Hundreds of goals do not achieve imperative level status and are never achieved. The simple fact is that senior management must assume that their orders will be carried out. In reality most are. But many fail and many are forgotten. Many only get lip service and many are changed, based on interpretation and the needs of the minute.

Virtually all projects that achieve senior level attention are reviewed and tracked, but a project that does not achieve this status may not get this attention. The history of projects in most companies shows that when projects are moved to the highest level of management attention, they tend to succeed. The success factor is thus senior-level attention.

Also important is the fact that projects tend to represent parts of a larger whole. Most can be considered to be part of some corporate objective or problem resolution. If this is not true, why spend the resources to do them? Few companies look at the work that is proposed as a composite whole. Few planners look at the work in terms of how it fits together to support corporate goals, and few companies view projects in this composite from a funding or product perspective. This type of vertical integration or alignment must be seriously considered. The benefits are a true picture of benefit, cost, effort, and disruption, and a way to make certain that the various business units are pulling together for the common advantage.

Assuming a review has taken place and the projects are meaningful and beneficial, then the question is, given the workload, can the business units really implement them? If the answer is no, and the projects are important, outside resources may be a reasonable alternative. But experience shows that cross-functional, cross-organizational projects are difficult to pull off. They require the close attention of senior-level management and the direct control of a formal senior-level sponsor.

Without this level of attention, it is questionable whether a project will be completed. Companies cancel, add, and change projects every day as needs change and the market direction moves. This is a sign of a responsive operation. But the impact and ripple effects of these changes must be reviewed and disseminated; changes and their results cannot be assumed to be common knowledge. They can, and do, make the overall objectives of another plan change, and the projects that support these other plans will fail unless they are realigned to suit.

Success in the implementation of any plan assumes that the goals are achievable. Clearly, goals should cause an organization to stretch and improve, but arbitrary goals and improper infrastructure support may result in a plan that cannot be accomplished. Many plans can fall into this category. The targets have no business case to back them up and the numbers are guesswork. If these numbers are easy to make, management gets lucky. If they can be made, they sometimes are. If they are a stretch, they are seldom made and if they are improbable, they are never made.

The solution is to assume very little in implementing a plan. Consistent success is not luck; it is based on a lot of homework and attention. Plans will be implemented only where they are reasonable, they are the right thing to do, and they are appropriately coordinated.

ASSUMPTION 6.7
STRATEGIC PLANS FLOW TO TACTICAL PLANS AND EVERY LEVEL SUPPORTS THE TACTICS.

The link between strategy and tactics is often theoretical at best. The strategy of a company can be viewed as a group of "whats" and the tactics as the "hows" for each "what." Assuming the "whats" are right, one must then look at the tactics needed to support them.

Once management agrees that the goals are not necessarily being imparted to everyone properly, the next consideration becomes the tactics of the business units. If the goals are not agreed upon, that is to say, are out of alignment, the tactics will also be out of sync. This causes a lot of money and time to be wasted in "spinning your wheels" work. Every company does it. An example of this situation is the case when everyone is running frantically from meeting to meeting every day. No one can schedule anything else unless it is three or four weeks in the future. No decisions are made and most meetings just produce more meetings. The questioning and proving and justifying go on indefinitely. Everyone is too busy and everyone needs more time and people. In this situation, strategy does not flow to tactics and tactics cannot be appropriately supported at all management and staff levels.

This situation was not invented for this book. Most companies have no shortage of meaningless meetings and false starts of programs. Too many projects are viewed as temporary, and management fails to follow through on recommendations and feedback.

These unproductive projects are acceptable if they are related to research or tests. Some tests will work out and some will not, but either way the goal is knowledge and the test should produce knowledge. However, when projects are not aligned to specific tactics and through them to specific corporate goals, they easily lose focus, direction, and support.

Tactics often change or are abandoned without any form of tieback to the strategy they support. Knowledge is lost. Over the course of a planning year, both the strategy and goals will change. Then the tactics that support them should also change. Unfortunately, unless effort is coordinated based on strategy and supporting tactics, any one of the three can change independently of the others. As the change continues over time, the original alignment of all three weakens and they become out of sync.

Where strategy is not aligned with tactics and work, belief in and commitment to the direction of the company will be questionable and the mobilization of management and the workforce toward accomplishing the corporate goals will be mostly words, with little action or effort.

Tactical alignment with corporate goals, with same-level tactics in different business units and with working tactics at lower levels, requires a firm understanding of the projects, the plans, and the direction of the company. This alignment allows the strategy to be translated into tactics and tactics into individual projects and then into tasks. It also identifies who is responsible for what part of the tactics and shows how they work together. In reality, a company's plan, its objectives, its tactics, and its projects combine in a type of puzzle to form a picture of the company for a given period of time. When pieces are missing, holes open up. When these holes exist, the company is at risk.

ASSUMPTION 6.8
IF PLANS ARE MET THE COMPANY WILL SUCCEED.

Clearly if a company's plans are successfully achieved, the company will succeed! If this is true, why do companies establish executive bonus targets, set production quotas, improve quality and cut costs, and then fail?

Planning, even formal planning, is approached differently in different companies. Some companies place great importance on the creation of strategic plans and little on the tactical plans that support them. Others use a bottom-up approach that builds from low-level business units to support a strategy only hinted at. Some are budget-driven and have little to do with real strategy and tactics. Most are a mix of all of these and more. But whatever approach is used, few managers think their planning is adequate. Surprisingly, most consulting firms think the plans they create for their clients are fine and are really used to manage the company.

Regardless of the overall approach, many plans are built in isolated components. These components often fail to fit together when viewed in total. Plans are giant multilevel puzzles. They take a variety of different views and levels of magnification to be understood. Very few companies take the time to align or "tune" their plans. Strategy does not flow to goals, goals do not flow to tactics, and tactics do not flow to projects. Project results are seldom viewed as either vertically or horizontally related to results of other projects. Each stands alone. In truth, planning in many companies is a task that is considered a waste of time: "No one follows the plan anyway; the only thing that's important is the budget."

It is likely in large companies that the success of one area will imply the failure of one or more others. This problem is seldom found in small companies. Small companies are generally run by a strong CEO and a very small group of senior managers who have direct control over every piece of the enterprise. They often create an informal plan and then meet periodically to make certain each unit is meeting its goals. In reality, that is all they need to do. In large companies, it is impossible for senior managers to have the type of hands-on, direct control that small company managers have. Here, senior managers must rely on summaries and financial reports obtained from layers of lower-level managers. They must count on these managers to accurately assess situations and the status of each project for them. They are isolated from the reality of the operation. Because of this span of control, it is not always possible for managers in different areas to identify disconnections or to find conflicts. And they do occur.

Many companies are also forced to take a short-term perspective by stockholders who want an immediate return on their investment. They are concerned solely about the next quarter and motivate the executive group accordingly. These goals are often less than farsighted and they can be damaging to the company's long-term viability.

> Several years ago, many railroads ran into financial trouble. In some countries they have now almost gone out of business. In an effort to strengthen the bottom line, several U.S. railroads began to sell property. Since most U.S. railroads owned a great deal of land, they were able to bring in quite a lot of money and show a profit. This was a short-term solution. They met their planned objectives by trading the future. They did not succeed in the long run.

The result of both short-term goals and misalignment of strategy to tactics is that many parts of the plan can succeed and yet the business can fail. Aside from a serious catastrophe, the company will first fail to meet strategic goals. This will often cause revenue problems, which will be met with short-term remedies.

Planning obviously works when approached properly. It is necessary for any company's long-term success. It cannot be taken for granted. It is quite possible for the plan to cause serious operational problems as uncoordinated project thrashing replaces orderly improvement. When companies spend the time to insure proper alignment, the plan's success has a much higher probability of leading to corporate success. But again, this cannot be assumed: many companies do not take the time to appropriately integrate the plan into the daily operation.

ASSUMPTION 6.9
PLANNING IS A ONCE-A-YEAR PROCESS. WE DO NOT CHANGE PLANS ONCE THEY ARE APPROVED AND BUDGETED.

At many companies (and almost every hospital), planning is considered to be a once-a-year activity. It is tied directly to the budget and once approved by the budget committee, it is cast in concrete. Quarterly or other reviews are really budget reviews and changes are not allowed. Managers are expected to live up to their estimates as approved in the budget.

But what happens when something significant changes? Any company or hospital is a dynamic entity that has a life of its own. It doesn't always behave as projected and external factors can often surprise corporate management. To paraphrase Murphy's law, "If it can happen it will and if it can't happen it may." It is still believed, however, that a good manager can manage to the plan, regardless of what externals change. It is simply not true in dynamic operations. But still the static budget and the static plan persist in many companies.

The evidence today is that planning and all the other recent attempts at improvement have been partially and inconsistently successful at best. The market has not waited, however. It has changed significantly and it continues to change at least hourly. The old approaches need to be improved and incorporated into the new ones. The resulting hybrid must be able to fit the corporate culture.

In most consistently successful companies, the planning process pervades the operation. It is part of all business activity. It is also a full-time, year-round effort. Managers assist one another in areas of overlap and the plans are continuously reviewed in light of the changing business operation and the market. This is challenging for many financial officers because the plan is never static. The budget is always evolving. Current financial information in these companies is critical: no small task considering the shape of financial systems in most companies.

The old approaches to planning—that often view planning as an annual necessity and that fail to insure both horizontal and vertical alignment through all levels of the company—are much easier to support than the currently appropriate type of planning. The investment in meaningful planning is high. The resistance will be high and the pressure to move back to the old ways will make any move to sound planning risky. This is inescapable. Managers must, however, acquire both the flexibility needed in today's market and a new approach to control. All resources must be mobilized as needed and investment and corporate direction must be capable of very rapid change, deployment, and redeployment.

The present state of corporate operation is that budgets and plans are flexible within limits. Even in companies with annual plans, government requirements, opportunity-based requirements, and problem resolutions cause change. Funding is found somewhere. But change is viewed as an isolated occurrence and the impact on the entire operation is seldom considered. Change is often not considered to be important enough to bring to everyone's attention, and few managers really understand how the master plan is being modified. The assumption is that senior management will let the people who need to know in on the secret. But many relationships are missed and many people who have a need to know are not notified. This is especially true of support services such as information systems.

To reflect the fast-paced global business market, planning must allow and support rapid change in direction, activity, and budgeting. Nothing can remain static and the static planning systems and approaches of the past are simply not appropriate for today or tomorrow. The fact is that planning must not only involve many more members of the company, but it must be done constantly. There is no longer a place for a single annual plan. Plans today must evolve continuously. A rolling approach that looks at months as a rolling year is needed. Through this approach, planning can change and evolve as the company changes.

While evolutive planning represents a significant change for many managers and companies, it is an important capability. The results are control, flexibility, and speed. The foundation for making any move in this direction begins with serious questioning of this and other planning assumptions.

ASSUMPTION 6.10
ALL MEASUREMENTS OF PERFORMANCE AGAINST PLANNED OBJECTIVES ARE BEING TRACKED FOR EVERY PART OF THE PLAN SOMEWHERE IN THE COMPANY.

Senior management must assume that performance against every strategy's goals, every tactic, and every project are being tracked somewhere in the company. Upper-level managers rely on financial and progress reports to identify problems and to show success. The quality of these reports is often considered suspect by these managers, but they are nonetheless their only contact with the real workings of the company. Because they have information summarized, it is assumed that the summaries are a roll-up of real metrics. As many managers honestly admit, this is a naive assumption. Few managers really have confidence in the metrics they are given.

One of the biggest reasons for problems in tracking is that objectives are individually interpreted based on the manager's own view. While in most companies no one group is responsible for pulling a common measurement system together, everyone assumes the various measurements will tie together. They may not.

The other cause of problems is the fact that metrics are not tied together into systems of interrelated calculations. Each metric stands alone in most companies. There is no attempt to review all the measurement activities or the things that are being measured. As discussed in Chapter 4, " Measurement: Managing the Business or Just Placing Blame?," companies tend to count a great many movements and totals. The problem is that many are relics of the past and do not support current information needs. Also, and possibly even worse, they cannot possibly provide the flexibility, quality, and reliability needed for the future. So even if it is assumed that all parts of a plan are being measured somewhere, it cannot be similarly assumed that the measurements are right or that quality is being built into the counts. Control is the usual driver in most current metric systems, not plan or project accountability. The metric systems in place may simply not be up to the challenges of today's information needs.

If one assumes that the metrics are appropriate, companies now run into another obstacle: the information services systems.

Few companies have the advantage of adequate computer support for metrics and planning. Again, as with manual metric calculations, the metrics available from automated systems are not integrated and are not based on composite comprehensive systems of interrelated metrics. The inability of computer groups to supply information on a cross-system basis has given rise to several executive information or decision support systems and to current technical concepts such as data mining and integrated data modeling. These efforts are in their infancy in most companies and it is too early to assess their worth.

Given the status of metric collection in most companies, it cannot be assumed that any factor is specifically being measured, or if it is, that the data can be converted to information or that information can be made available in an integrated manner.

ASSUMPTION 6.11
PLANNING IS A SENIOR MANAGEMENT ACTIVITY.

Many managers at all levels assume that planning is a senior management activity, with the ancillary participation of a few internal consultants and other planning staff to help them. Mid-level and line managers seldom contribute to these planning processes. The belief that strategy and planning must be cloaked in secrecy is now being challenged by a new wave of strategy experts. While their approaches are each different, the common theme is that strategy must be taken out into the corporate light and exposed to a variety of people to obtain a fruitful result. This exposure is critical and the lack of it is a major reason for the failures of planning in the past—although virtually no consulting firm will admit to past planning failures in the companies they assist.

The reasons for the secrecy of the past are varied and must be examined in light of today's need for creativity, insight, and operational improvement. The fact is that senior managers do not have all the insight and answers in a company. They do not have all the creativity and operational knowledge. They also do not have a corner on customer insight and market understanding. Based on this recognition and a belief that their plans are confidential but mostly not top secret, many companies have started to expand their real planning activity. This expansion allows the high-level plans and the department plans to be linked, in many companies for the first time. With this linking it is possible for everyone to know what is going on.

The disconnection between strategy, tactics, plans, and budgets of the past was based on this old assumption. Separate groups worked to build their parts of the overall corporate plan as indicated in the "guide." This guide usually was and is an unintegrated group of documents that are typically not even published together. With this lack of focus and coordination, strategy cannot be implemented. The organization thrashes as individual interests and interpretations guide operations. Reporting against the plan may seem to show adequate progress, but often the reports are constructed to show what many want to prove or what they believe senior management wants to hear. Without a way to tie activity together, no other option is available.

Today new approaches, techniques, and tools allow the integration of planning levels and the alignment of activity and products. The use of these methods is a challenge to this assumption. They remove the responsibility for strategy and planning from senior management and distribute it throughout the organization and even to the customers and the suppliers. This extended planning group offers the input of multiple views and ideas. The limited role of strategy and planning can and should now be changed. Change can only be initiated by challenging the past and its assumptions and value systems.

CHALLENGING ASSUMPTIONS IN PLANNING

A significant movement has started that seems to be heading backwards into the past trends of management science. Companies are rediscovering the need to plan and to strategize. The years of downsizing have taken their toll. Companies now see themselves as lean and mean. They feel they are now ready for the future. While this is unlikely to be true for most companies, many believe they are now better able to compete and they are looking for ways to move forward. While the bloodletting is still going on in many organizations, it is clear that companies must change from the past approaches and markets regardless of whether they are ready or not.

Companies are looking at their strategies and many are recognizing that the strategies of the past must be replaced. Several new strategy experts are emerging, and along with them there are several new approaches to creating strategy, including value-based evaluation, discussed in Chapter 9, "Cost vs. Value." But again many theorists, academics, and managers forget one important fact: once management sees the goal or strategy they must be able to formulate the tactics and plans needed to get there. Then they must actually make certain that the resources are available to do the needed work and weave it all together into a cohesive fabric that moves the company.

In this chapter we have discussed the views of success that must all be taken into account and several of the assumptions that must be challenged in order to move forward. The fact is that the ability to accurately plan and then carry through has been seriously hurt in most companies. The ranks of the people who were once responsible for these activities have been eliminated in many companies and reduced in others. Planning groups have been decimated and middle management, the project leaders, has been significantly reduced. These skills must be redeveloped quickly for companies to succeed. The unfortunate fact is that most companies downsized too much in vital areas that were mistakenly considered to be unimportant.

Creativity is needed in dealing with this issue. While it is vital to extend the planning activity beyond the hallowed corporate ex-

ecutive suites, it is also important to recreate the skills needed to do
something about the plan. Someone must implement it. It will not
happen by mandate or threat. Senior management should seek
competent project leaders and put a structure in place to align and
manage activities, including projects and problem resolution. These
people are the missing link that downsizing has created. They can
be placed in a separate structure parallel to operations and be considered the change agents of the future. Corporate budgets reflect
the cutbacks. They should not be allowed to grow needlessly or
companies will be back where they were before the past several
painful years. The best human resources must be placed in positions that maximize the use of their skills. This is not necessarily in
the operational areas. Really creative thinkers should be moved to
the project teams. These teams must be intimately in tune with the
business operational units. They must also have the skills to continuously improve those operations through sound detail-level planning, close operational interaction, and budget justification.

EFFECTIVE PLANNING

Several books on strategic planning have recently been published.
Apparently process reengineering and quality are old topics and
the quest for new material has caused business writers to begin to
recycle concepts. Articles on planning have become more frequent
and are gaining notice and support among senior managers. The
old, persistent assumptions discussed in this chapter, however, will
continue to make planning ineffective. Regardless of the different
spins one uses to modify planning processes, the fact still remains
that the process will not succeed unless management challenges
the assumptions that surround their traditional and even their new
planning processes.

Several steps are needed to make planning effective, from the executive levels of the business all the way down to the working levels.

1. Corporate planning should be expanded to include operational,
   research, sales, and line managers. These lower-level managers
   can provide valuable detailed information about feasibility and

about the immediate problems of the business that may not be apparent to senior managers and high-level planning staff.

2. The strategy must be tied clearly and directly to the tactics needed to support it, and also to the change projects that will produce the actual working-level improvements.

3. Everyone in the company who is affected by the company's plans should be mobilized to support the change projects, new work flows, and, where appropriate, the overall strategy.

4. Everyone in the company should understand how they fit into the corporate plan, the teams working on the plan, and its change projects. They should also understand why their jobs are important. They all must believe that their contributions are needed to make the company succeed.

5. The plans must be formalized and the formal business plan must be enforced rigorously.

6. Some form of bottom-up organization development approach should be implemented to provide real participation throughout the company, and commitment to the goals and new improvement ideas.

7. The company's informal planning method must be either eliminated or institutionalized so that there is only one planning and change methodology. This methodology should be thoroughly documented and understood throughout the company.

Each of these actions has been proven to contribute to successful planning and execution of the plan, but each has its price. Planning is as big a problem today as ever. It is also as big a problem in big companies as in smaller ones. The planning effort costs companies millions each year and there is seldom much gained from it. Past approaches simply have not been effective. However, now that other approaches to gaining control have met with mixed success, many companies are taking a step back and placing their bets again on their strategy and plans.

The reasons for the high failure rate in process improvement and quality improvement efforts have little to do with the validity of the concepts. Like past planning efforts, the problems are usually found in inadequately trained staff, poor execution, and hidden agendas. The assumptions discussed in this chapter address some of the basic reasons why planning fails. Until these assumptions and others that may be unique to a company are challenged, planning will continue to provide mixed results.

MAKING THE FORMAL PLAN WORK

There are two major drawbacks to successful planning. First, getting everyone in the business committed to the process (or "engaged" in change) is hard. Second, sound, comprehensive planning is a lot of work. There is a real shortage of staff in most operations. Who will have the time to plan? Who will monitor the planning process? The questions could go on for pages.

Unfortunately, the answers are not what most managers want to hear. The planning function is critically important. It needs to be in place and it needs to be staffed properly. But it also needs to be overhauled or reengineered in a majority of companies. Planning activities have been given less attention in the recent past as corporate focus shifted to quality improvement, cost cutting, downsizing, and process improvement. The cost in terms of planning has been an erosion both of planning's importance and the ability of companies to anticipate the direction of the market and to begin to plan a response to customer buying trends. Certainly the current move to once again emphasize the "big thinking" strategic approach is a rebound effect from the lack of focus on the future. The positive part of this past trend is a greater understanding of the need to involve more people in the planning process. The other positive outcome from the reemphasis on planning is the concept of market creation and manipulation. Many companies are looking at how they can find new untapped markets and how they can reposition their old product lines or new product lines to address these opportunities. The recent emphasis on planning is critical to long-term success. But here arises the new challenge: planning itself must be reengineered.

This reengineering begins with several fundamental questions that many managers will not want to answer. For example, each business unit must define what it really does and what value that brings to the company. If there is not a reason to keep the business unit, remove it. The same goes for any person who does not have the skills the operation needs. Retrain them or find replacements. The productive approach is to modify the planning or change system so that all employees, or at least most employees, win. Once this is accepted, the company and its planning processes will have a chance to succeed.

The threat of planning commitment is also a problem for most companies. Once committed to the plan, a manager will be responsible for specific end products. Many managers really do not want this level of personal responsibility or exposure. To address this and the other problems involved in creating a new and revitalized planning process, the assumptions discussed in this chapter and many others must be questioned. The traditional answers must be challenged.

INSTITUTIONALIZING THE INFORMAL PROCESS

Most companies actually manage change not by a formal methodology, nor under the guidance of the annual plan, but on an informal project-by-project basis. Each project is authorized and funded on its own merits and is only attached to the annual plan by pure rationalization. Projects are assigned a high-level sponsor, who plans the project and executes it with direct support from the CEO. The project team creates a simple time line (a Gantt chart) and reports its progress at a series of special meetings and also at some of the regularly scheduled senior management meetings.

It is common to find a business with two planning and change methodologies: a formal one based upon a structured planning process and an informal one. Most strategic planning consultation and advice focuses on the formal process: making it better and making it work. However, there is another choice. The informal process can be institutionalized, and can replace the formal one as the company's principal approach to change. In most cases, it already has done so. The project-by-project approach can be recognized as the chief change approach of the company, and a series of projects can become the only annual change plan that the company uses. It is crude, but it works.

In any case, planning is critical to the success of a business. The company's approach, annual plan, and project plans should be thoroughly communicated from top to bottom and every phase of them should be tracked. Some special methods should be used to obtain (and test) the commitment of every person in the company who is involved, and that should be every person in the company.

ORGANIZATION DEVELOPMENT

Engagement and commitment are easier when a bottom-up approach is used, but this does not lend itself to radical changes in the business. While it does infuse new ideas and perspectives into the strategy and planning processes, there is at least the perception of a loss of management control. As a result, organization development (OD, or any of its variants, such as action research) is not universally accepted despite its famous successes. The most often cited example of OD working as it should is the Volvo plant experience at Kalmar, where the assembly line was replaced by a process of assembling cars from the ground up by small groups, increasing both productivity and quality.

It is possible to incorporate OD into a traditional top-down hierarchy. The method is simple: senior management sets goals and a vision and then OD takes over. The shop floor democracy approach is used to invite the working levels either to decide how they would fulfill the objectives that management has suggested, or to change them and come up with a better vision. Senior management can't lose: the worst that can happen is the working levels agreeing that they can't do better than what has been laid out for them. In this way, the advantages of a bottom-up approach can be combined with those of a top-down approach.

There are probably many other ways to arrive at this happy combination, and it is worthwhile to try one, for the sake of a much improved level of worker commitment as well as better business plans.

THE RIGHT APPROACH FOR THE FUTURE

The following approach is based on process improvement and strategic impact. It involves an analysis of the current marketplace to define opportunity, and also strategy and business modeling to insure organizational and process alignment for problem definition and improvement. Clearly, work must be related to one of three things: it must move the company toward the attainment of strategic goals, it must correct a problem, or it must improve the operation. A fourth type of work is obviously the simple continuation of the operation. Business must continue while strategy is being created and improvements are being applied to the operation.

Personal interest must also be considered to be a critical factor in any planning. Management must work to insure that personal interests will be served by the company's success. In the past, secrecy was the device used for keeping people guessing and, consequently, presumably unable to fulfill individual hidden agendas. Planning was discussed on a need-to-know basis and most people were left out of the process. Today, this secrecy cannot be continued. It is simply too limiting. The problem is thus how to channel personal interests. While the answer varies from company to company depending on culture and on management's commitment and strength, it is important to identify productive and nonproductive personnel and to work with the less productive to insure that their personal fulfillment is tied to the company's success.

BUDGET VARIANCES AND PLANNING

In companies everywhere, plans and projects are constantly being shifted and canceled. Budgets are currently being set aggressively, so shortfalls are a common occurrence. When budget variances occur, the first response is to cut expenses, often in areas other than those that are over the budget. External resources are an easy target, and so are change projects. When budget repairs kill projects, the results are very negative, usually worse than anticipated. In fact, anything that causes projects to be canceled must be considered a negative influence on the company. The simple fact is that if the project was worth doing, it should be finished. If it can be canceled or delayed, it should not have been approved in the first place—either it is important or it is not. Management needs to reconsider the age-old belief that efforts can just be cut if the overall department or corporate budget looks as if it will exceed approved amounts.

Budget variances are telling a story. The response of stopping progress to hold the variance level is not acceptable. This is a knee-jerk financial response: it does not help the company to improve quality, competitive position, or market. The variance story is rather a pointer either to mismanagement or to the effect of unpredicted external factors. In the future, the flexibility needed to move quickly to take advantage of opportunities will require a very different perspective on budget variance. Variance will be a sign of flexibility in most instances and not necessarily a sign of mismanagement or poor planning. The key will be getting everyone to understand what is really going on in the company.

In many cases today, project budgets are eaten by increased staffing as managers shift money and move to implement "work-arounds" to computer system inadequacies or to procedure problems. The results of these moves are an increasing staffing burden, a delay in improvement, and a lack of flexibility. The real problems should be addressed, rather than applying short-term symptom relief.

While today's production needs are clearly the foundation for success or profit, the change projects of the company are its future. The tradeoff is thus the present for the future.

In addition to project cancellations due to budget variances, many efforts are canceled due to budget wars. In this case no one is willing to contribute to the continuation of the effort. It simply does not provide adequate personal advantage. The following example was provided by Timothy Bremer.

As a result of a business process reengineering firm's efforts through an initial three-week review of customer service operations conducted for its client, a billion-dollar international manufacturer, the client company decided to proceed. The next steps included a six-week analysis of work activities in five key areas of the business (procurement, inventory, order processing, manufacturing, and information technology). More than 20 consultants and 30 of the client's internal management staff were mobilized to support five teams in this effort. They were also to review operations within three of the client's divisions. At least eight plants, located in as many cities across the U.S., were visited by the work teams.

At the conclusion of the analysis, significant multimillion-dollar savings were identified. The company even employed the services of professional filmmakers to capture the essence of the client/consultant teams' findings, and to prepare a video that was going to be sent to all the client's U.S. locations as an introduction, communication, and kick-off for the next phase of this major project.

Everything was on target for the teams to begin the design and development of the improved processes, but someone forgot a key element. There was no agreement as to how the effort's funding was going to be split between the European parent company and the U.S. locations. As a result of not being able to come to agreement on how the funding would be supported and other "political" maneuvering between the entities, the project was aborted, and its projected savings were lost. The company managers and staff who worked on the project were deeply disappointed, and to a considerable degree lost their respect for the company's senior management.

PLANS AND VISIONS

If there is a single lesson to be learned from the success stories of the past twenty years of business, it is that bold approaches to business are more important than raw technological innovation. The vision of a truly gifted business mind is the most important factor in planning. Any methodology should recognize this by encouraging creativity among the leaders of the business, and then assuring that the visions they develop come to pass. Starting with an obvious objective, like increasing stockholder equity or beating the competition, will lead a business to mediocrity at best. There is no need to assume that survival is the best a business can hope for in the age of global competition. Just don't do it.

C H A P T E R
S E V E N

INFORMATION TECHNOLOGY

CAN INFORMATION TECHNOLOGY REALLY IMPROVE THE BOTTOM LINE?

Information technology (I/T) has come through many generations in business, and has to a large degree shed the mystery that once surrounded it. However, information technology and the staff who support it are still not fully trusted by business. The concept of using a mainframe system is under fire and the actual benefit of information technology, both centralized and on the desktop, is being seriously questioned. Computer technology is a business function under siege. The typical large business computer group is concerned with continual budget cuts, increasingly unmanageable systems maintenance requirements, attacks from end users who believe that they can do it better themselves, and technology advancement that continues to outpace anyone's ability to use or manage it. The situation is beyond the ability of experts; what chance does a business manager have in dealing with it? How can business evaluate technology's contribution and use it effectively?

The first step, we suggest, is clearer scrutiny. Challenge the assumptions, strip away the last vestiges of myth and mystique, and proceed objectively in the interest of the bottom line. In this chapter, we will have a look at the assumptions behind some of the problems in this, possibly the most commonly dysfunctional area in business today.

183

First, a little history. To understand why there are so many un-challenged assumptions about information technology, it is necessary to go back to its beginnings and trace its development to the present.

Information technology started over a century ago, invented by Herman Hollerith in the form of punched cards to assist in taking the U.S. census. I/T grew slowly in business as improved tabulating equipment was built to process the punched cards, and was greatly accelerated by the introduction of the stored program digital com-puter at the end of World War II. But from its inception until the early 1970s, information technology was oriented around the punched card, and this limitation shaped its use. Punched cards were seldom processed one at a time. To make automation function at all in business, the cards and the transactions they represented had to be batched, and processed in groups. The result of the processing was printed reports. Batch processing with paper reporting was common in business from the 1930s, and it still exists. It was the way of busi-ness long enough for it to become habit. Batch processing provided the basis for some assumptions that are still accepted without being consciously considered in today's business world.

When generations of computers are discussed, the reference is usually to the basic technology of the computer hardware. The first generation were vacuum tube computers, the second were transis-torized, the third used large-scale integration on chips. However, these generations are not as meaningful to business as the ones concerned with the actual function of computers. The first gener-ation was the one described above, the age of the punched card and the batch process. The next generation of computer use began in the early 1970s with the development of the on-line system, which used a computer terminal linked directly, or remotely via telephone lines, to a mainframe computer. This dramatically changed the way a computer could be used.

The age of on-line computer systems made possible the pro-cessing of transactions one by one as they are presented to the company, or even as they actually occur in some cases. Taking an order over the telephone and processing it as it is being taken is an example of this real-time mode. Quite suddenly, there was no longer a need to wait until the end of the month to do everything. Business has been slow to realize the benefits of this capability, but the results are not doubted by anyone today.

Unfortunately, another pattern emerged in business with the on-line age. The ability of management to control and exploit the technology fell behind the pace of hardware evolution to a significant extent, and management has not caught up to this day. This problem has caused more of the trouble that information technology has had in the business world than any other single factor.

We have now reached the third generation of computer use and perhaps the fourth. The technology essential for the third generation was the personal computer, and its business impact has been end user computing in all its forms. (Another common term for the use of technology in business is distributed processing, but that is just one form of end user computing.) Since this generation is still developing, a fully objective historical perspective of its impact is not yet available. Despite the penetration of the personal computer into business, its use has not matured.

The personal computer is also responsible for what seems to be another generation, whose identifying feature is global networking. The Internet today is still used as a toy, and not a very constructive one, in most businesses. The business potential of extended network capabilities is still unknown, but the technology can be purchased by anyone. It is possible in many businesses for an individual staff member to use the Internet without any management control. Thus the trend of decreasing ability to manage information technology continues to the present day. It may get worse before it gets better.

The struggle between the requirement to gain or maintain control over information technology—for the sake of maintaining some vestige of information security, to say nothing of controlling the costs of technology—and empowering staff to do their jobs as well as possible is found in almost every large company.

THE TECHNOLOGY DISADVANTAGED COMPANY

Despite technology's turbulent history and rapid rate of change, some companies today make much better use of technology than others. Some make a distinct competitive advantage of it. Others are so mired in old systems and manage computing so badly that they are what we call "technology disadvantaged." The outward signs of being technology disadvantaged are easy to spot. Most obvious is an enormous backlog of requests to change the computer systems, generated by business people trying in vain to remove the obstacles to getting their work done. Other signs include a bitterly adversarial relationship between technicians and business operations staff. In general, the attitude toward central systems is one of distrust, with many operations staff seeking end user alternatives. In most technology disadvantaged companies, the business operations staff regards the computer systems as immutable obstacles; any systems change is considered a significant effort, requiring executive approval.

Technology disadvantaged companies have a particular need to revise their approach to managing information and its supporting technology, but they also have particularly great difficulty in doing so. Just to discuss I/T in these companies is a real problem. It is the basic paradigms and assumptions related to information technology that lock these businesses into their present positions.

INFORMATION TECHNOLOGY ASSUMPTIONS

The following are ten of the most prevalent assumptions about information technology being made in business at the present time. As in other chapters, it should not be inferred that any one person or company makes all of these assumptions; indeed in the case of information technology, many of the assumptions conflict directly with others. But that is part of the peculiar nature of the business use of computers.

ASSUMPTION 7.1
INFORMATION TECHNOLOGY HAS NEVER WORKED AND WILL NEVER WORK.

This is an extreme view, but it is surprisingly common. Some business people truly believe computers are just a replacement for clerical labor, and may not even be cost effective. This opinion is usually well concealed, since it seems old-fashioned and is almost guaranteed to make a negative impression. This assumption is very difficult to challenge, but, paradoxically, it may inspire a healthy skepticism toward information technology that should actually be encouraged in the right circumstances.

A business person who feels technology is a fad whose net contribution is negative is, as a rule, one who has not often been in the mainstream of computer use. It is still not unusual to find managers and senior staff who have come up the through ranks of large businesses without ever actually using a computer. Many of them have suffered from computer failures, which have unfortunately been all too common for the last thirty years. Severe critics of information technology are generally also found in technology disadvantaged companies, companies in which business processes are actually impeded by computer systems.

One place where this assumption would not be expected is in the computer industry itself. However, surprising as it may seem, the use of computing did not become widespread in sales support for computers until many other industries were using it. Now, of course, every computer company uses computers to support their own sales efforts.

A story about this assumption comes from the West Coast where a large financial services company (which later developed an enviable reputation for using technology effectively) got off to a very slow start. Like most other companies in its industry, this company put its first computer into the punched card tabulating shop. It was an IBM 650, the first commercially successful computer. IBM itself was responsible for much of the programming of the new machine, which just augmented the tabulating equipment. Cards went into the computer, and new cards came out. The only new advantage was that the computer could perform more complex calculations than the punch card tabulating machines that it augmented (in this case the company had a large number of IBM 407s.) The new machine was under the control of the head of the tabulating department, who was not even an officer of the company. There was nothing unusual in any of this; it was all typical of the industry at the time. However, as the company's use of the computer become more significant, the computing organization stayed basically the same, reporting to a department head, who reported to an assistant vice president, who reported to a vice president, who reported to the senior vice president for finance, the company's CFO. The computer remained buried at this level for the next twenty years. At the dawn of the on-line generation, all of automation still reported to a department head in finance. The budget was larger than that of any vice president in the company, but the entire senior management corps of the company considered computers mere technical support, and that only when they worked perfectly. The company was forced to go through a major reorganization before it could update its computer support so that it could continue to compete, during which time its market position suffered.

To some extent, the assumption that computers are not worth senior management's bothering with continues to this day, and is responsible for making some companies technology disadvantaged. However, this assumption is not as dangerous as assuming that computers can do anything (as we discuss in some of the other assumptions). The trick is to have a healthy skepticism, but to be open to letting technology provide real advantages where they can be had without undue risk. The first step is analyzing the unchallenged assumptions, so that attitudes that stand in the way of objectivity can be set aside.

ASSUMPTION 7.2
ALL COMPUTER SYSTEMS ARE USED POORLY; THE USERS
DON'T REALLY KNOW THE SYSTEMS.

This is a technician's assumption, and it is often presented by the information systems department through the chief information officer to the senior executives of the business. The senior executives seldom question it, but they should. It is almost never true.

Business users of systems do not often have detailed knowledge of the precise technical aspects of what they are using, but they are more often than not very highly expert in how to actually use the technology to support their own work. It is a matter of survival; if they do not learn the systems, they cannot do their jobs. Often they know how the systems work better than the technicians assigned to maintain them. Some users become more knowledgeable than others and their expertise becomes well known among their peers. There are always some users, new ones and recalcitrant ones, who do not manage to learn the systems, and it is quite natural that technicians are more aware of their level of skill than that of the expert users, since these few slackers cause most of the problems. The technicians' view is therefore greatly skewed, and they seldom get to know their users well enough to correct it.

This assumption leads to a surprising number of information technology's problems in business. Not only does it lead to poor relationships between technicians and operations staff, but it creates a very unrealistic target for the technology support in many businesses.

An illustrative case occurred in a mid-Atlantic bank. At the time a fairly stable work force had developed many long-standing relationships between technical staff and operations personnel at the working level. Most systems technicians had a small group of contacts, made over several years of helping them. These contacts were valued by the management of the systems department, who used them as touchstones for new ideas and as an informal source of user satisfaction data. It was assumed that the contacts were the best users, while actually they were among the worst. Much of the bank's new technology support was targeted at the low end of the user community, which required more help and thus increased the overall cost of information technology in the bank. One particular difficulty occurred when the bank looked into purchasing a customer information system to replace their old, internally written one. This investigation occurred early in the history of purchased banking systems, when it would have been much easier to convert to such a system than it is today. However, the network of contacts gave uniformly negative opinions, which influenced the bank to lose a splendid opportunity. They finally discovered their error when the design of a major systems change was formally and widely reviewed by operations and rejected because it made too many concessions to inept users. Good computer systems help good people do their work better. They do not compensate for bad work.

ASSUMPTION 7.3
WE KEEP SPENDING MORE ON INFORMATION
TECHNOLOGY, BUT WE NEVER GET MORE OUT OF IT.

This assumption is related to the first, that information technology does not work at all, but differs in that it specifically refers to budgeting and directing resources to information technology. The assumption that is made is not as strong as saying that technology never works, it is just saying that incremental investments in technology do not change the apparent level of support provided by the technology, nor the satisfaction of the users, nor the company's competitive position, nor the bottom line.

This assumption, whether it is held consciously and vociferously or unconsciously and secretly, is usually caused by the lack of any demonstrable connection between computer investments and the returns from computer investments. Traditionally, there is some sort of cost justification for most major systems development efforts, but much of the technology in use in business today seems to have gotten in the back door. Mainframes are installed and upgraded based on predicted demand rather than the effect the expense will have on overall corporate profit. Local area networks are justified by very soft analysis, if any. Unfortunately, this assumption is often based on fact, or perhaps it is more accurate to say lack of fact.

There have been many efforts to identify the real business benefits of computing. It would seem to be advantageous for companies that sell computers to be able to demonstrate their benefits in precise quantities, but none has ever offered this service. The only help a business has today are the few associations and consulting firms that specialize in comparative statistics for large computer facilities. A company may subscribe to one of these agencies and provide its computer size and use figures and receive in return a set of well-presented graphs showing how they compare with all other subscribers, as well as with companies in their own industries and geographic areas. There are also comparators published by some trade associations. However, as things stand today, businesses are very much on their own when they address the problem of measuring the actual contribution that information technology makes to the bottom line. In the absence of reliable numbers, the assumption that incremental investments in information technology may not create any benefit will be made, and so far cannot be challenged.

ASSUMPTION 7.4
THE INFORMATION TECHNOLOGY BACKLOG IS TYPICAL AND UNAVOIDABLE.

During the great era of systems development, most large organizations built staggering inventories of special systems, many of which do common business functions, but of course they all do them differently. There are probably over 10,000 ordering systems in the United States alone, and most of them are second or third generation systems. They all do much the same thing. Most banks have their own customer information systems. Almost all insurance companies have written their own claims systems. So virtually every business has an enormous number of systems, programs, files, databases, and job controls. All of them must be maintained. Computer systems maintenance is the least desirable job in the computer professions and has almost never been done well. Systems are usually not very well written, organized, or documented, and poor maintenance makes them degenerate continually.

It would seem that backlogs are unavoidable, and they indeed are if the overall requirement of providing effective technology support for business processes is approached as it has been in the past. However, it is these old approaches that have created the backlogs, and the same approaches make them continue to grow. There is nothing in the basic nature of information technology that requires a backlog of unfulfilled improvement requests.

There are a number of ways to attack a backlog. A few that have been used and proven in many companies are:

- Putting systems requests on a full chargeback basis, allowing anyone to have any change very quickly, if they are willing to pay for the changes (in most cases, the charges are very high).
- Getting outside resources to make the changes (control can be a problem).
- Deleting any change request from the backlog that has not been acted upon in six months.
- Creating a "model office" to manage the changes to both computer systems and the business functions they support. Model

offices are well known in the insurance industry, where they have had a proven impact on rationalizing changes to systems and making the best use of available technologies.

- Documenting the current systems to help speed all changes, although this is often seen as having no immediate return (and also as investing in obsolete systems) and therefore is seldom seriously recommended.

There are occasionally some very creative approaches to altering old "legacy" systems. Here is one example.

A new chief information officer (hired from the outside by a financial services business) analyzed the daunting backlog of change requests he inherited and saw that many of them addressed a common goal: providing on-line information to customer service representatives to support immediate telephone inquiries. Rather than modify all of the old systems, he initiated the creation of what would come to be called a data warehouse, although this one was somewhat specialized. He simply had a single program written that tied many of the legacy systems together. This rather modest new system not only wiped out some of the more pressing line items in his backlog, but also precluded many new requests that would have swelled it further.

ASSUMPTION 7.5
IF WE JUST GET A NEW COMPUTER (OR SOFTWARE),
EVERYTHING WILL IMPROVE.

The opposite of assuming that computers are no good is assuming that computers are omnipotent. Of course, no reasonable person consciously assumes either of these extremes fully and no one holds both opinions at the same time. But both can (and do) coexist in the same company, and both are barriers to effective information technology decisions.

This assumption, we are embarrassed to report, can often result from the efforts of our colleagues in the consulting business. Too often, the result of a consulting engagement is a recommendation to install new technology. The justification is often compelling, but there is seldom a hard prediction of bottom-line benefits made to support it. It is a very safe recommendation for a consultant to make, since few companies will undertake a major technology installation in response to a consultant's report, and then if the consultant has not solved the company's problems, the company has only itself to blame. Here is an example.

A California insurance company hired a prestigious consulting firm to reengineer a core business process. The engagement took eight months and over a dozen people were sent to every part of the company to research the real requirements of the business. The current process was not mapped, because the consulting firm followed the advice of Michael Hammer and began with a blank sheet of paper. The final recommendation of the study was that the company install a local area network. After all the presentations were made and the congratulations died down, the company was at a loss as to how to take specific action. In the end, nothing whatever was done. The cost of the study was several million dollars, but more important was the lost time, over eight months in which real work could have been done.

Another motivation for assuming new technology will work wonders is the widespread belief that the most progressive and profitable companies are using technology better than anyone else. There is some truth in that. Technology is the most important change instigator in our civilization and in business as well. However, some of the world's most profitable companies, such as Kraft

Foods, are not known as technology innovators. Kraft, for example, is not a leader in electronic document interchange (EDI), nor is it able to supply its distributors as quickly as some of its competition. Kraft, unlike some other corporate giants like Sears, has never been known for buying every new machine on the market. But Kraft is very profitable. On the reverse side of the coin, Northwest Airlines pioneered the use of image processing for ticket post-processing. The system works well and has saved Northwest significant process expenses, but the airline has not risen to a position of dominance in its industry as a result of it. Computing, even when it is doing its best, is only one factor among many in business.

Chasing this assumption down requires a company to develop methods for determining the benefit of information technology. This is not impossible, but it is not easy. The first step is understanding that technology supports the process or work of a business, whether it is used for decisions (like a credit check) or the information is just part of the work (like putting a customer's address on a shipping label). This means that if the company can measure the costs of its business processes, and it can predict the change in costs that applying technology can bring about, it can compute the bottom-line potential of the technology. The technology itself, without consideration for how it is used, has no benefit at all—just cost (and lots of cost, in most cases).

ASSUMPTION 7.6
IF THE MAINFRAME COMPUTER CAN BE REPLACED, EVERYTHING WILL BE CHEAPER AND MORE USER-FRIENDLY, BECAUSE PCS ARE CHEAPER AND MORE USER-FRIENDLY THAN MAINFRAMES.

The rise first of minicomputers and more recently of personal computers have put the use of mainframes in question. The questions, however, are not always the right ones. It is sometimes appropriate to replace mainframes with cheaper and more effective alternatives, but not always, and forcing the issue can lead to impairing an entire business. The root of this assumption is usually a long-standing distrust of the mainframe system and the central information technology staff. In most cases, getting rid of the perceived tyrannical and arrogant mainframe computer technician is the most important motivation.

A closely related assumption is that information technology ought to be decentralized or outsourced. There are companies that have gone in both directions, first decentralizing, then recentralizing, or outsourcing and then moving the systems back in-house. All of these actions are intended to relieve either management or users of the pain of dealing with the information technology group, and they are all in vain. The responsibility for how well the company does its work, including how well the work is supported by technology, ultimately falls upon the most senior management of any business. Avoiding the requirement to be directly involved in technology decisions only passes the buck, and probably passes it to someone who is less than fully committed to the primary goals of the business. No matter how information technology is configured, mainframe or personal computer network, it must always be managed. At the present time, managing a network of PCs is much more difficult in many respects than managing a mainframe.

There is another interesting example of this assumption at work. The meteoric growth of SAP, a German-based company that sells computer software that covers much of the operational support and accounting functions of medium to large businesses, can be at least partially attributed to the desire to just get away from large mainframes. Release 3 of their software moved from the mainframe to a computer network using personal computers and high-powered network servers—a client/server or distributed system. The PCs are the clients and the network server workstations provide data and processing services for them. The popularity of Release 3 was unanticipated. Although SAP is an attractive system in it own right, much of the vigor of Release 3 was due to it reducing its customers' reliance on their mainframes. SAP clients put up with a somewhat less powerful tool than in the prior releases, and the traumatic conversion that all versions of SAP require, to obtain this feature. Other software vendors cannot fail to notice this, and although it will take a few years for them to catch up, there will soon be many software products that will emphasize migration off of mainframe computers. This assumption is very difficult to challenge, since it is based on a somewhat emotional response to the technology.

ASSUMPTION 7.7
IT IS CHEAPER TO CONTINUE TO FIX THE CURRENT INFORMATION TECHNOLOGY ENVIRONMENT THAN TO REPLACE IT.

The huge inventory of home-built computer systems that most medium and large organizations rely upon—called legacy systems—are uniformly troublesome throughout the business world. If a company is technology disadvantaged, old systems are usually the cause. Old systems are costly to maintain, changing them requires too much time to keep up with the business, and they generally do not support the daily operational requirements of the company. Despite this, most large companies put up with a large inventory of legacy systems. The assumption is made that since the cumulative cost of building the current systems was some overwhelmingly large amount, it will not be possible to replace them. For some companies in the financial services industries (in general, financial services spends the highest fraction of its budget on information technology), the cumulative investment in computer software development is several hundred million dollars, costs that today seem an insurmountable barrier to replacement.

This assumption is one that can and must be challenged. There are several factors that make this both necessary and feasible. First, legacy systems cost more to maintain than to replace. It is widely accepted that 80 percent of the cost of software is not in development, but in maintenance. Any software can be replaced at less cost than to maintain it, if the following guidelines are observed:

1. The software development costs must be capitalized and depreciated over a realistic time period. Much software that was built in the seventies was justifiably depreciated over three years, the reason being that the technology was advancing so quickly that it would be obsolete after that. It indeed became obsolete, but that did not take it out of service. In most cases, software built ten and twenty years ago is still in service.

2. The software must be built right and fully documented. Today's methods support somewhat cheaper development costs, and

far cheaper maintenance after the system is finished, but only if the process is not rushed and steps like documentation control are not skipped.

3. The business process should be analyzed and revised for the new systems. Lack of detailed knowledge of how the business works inflates the cost of software development. In the face of doubt, a software designer or programmer is forced to write code to take care of more variability than necessary. Most systems are twice as large as they need to be. Additionally, this guideline will assure that the finished product actually meets the demands of the business, and that the workflow supported is altered to take advantage of the new technology.

Using conservative methods (computer aided software engineering, or CASE tools, available for over ten years), it will cost less for most companies to replace their debilitating old software than to live with it.

Second, there are methods other than redevelopment that may be used to make the replacement process even less expensive. Our own Evolutive Technology, described at the end of this chapter, is one such alternative. Another is buying general purpose systems, such as SAP. Once this assumption is seriously challenged, it should be possible to identify many alternatives to living with unacceptable information technology systems. Just don't do it.

ASSUMPTION 7.8
THE MOST IMPORTANT FACTOR IN BUSINESS IS DATA. IF WE CAN GET THE RIGHT DATA TO THE RIGHT PLACE AT THE RIGHT TIME, THE BUSINESS WILL SUCCEED.

This assumption is made by the peculiar breed of information technology technicians who are concerned with data. They occupied the limelight of data processing in the early 1980s, and have yet to accept the limitations of their craft in supporting business operations and decision making. They have formed a view of business centered around their own specialty. They are hardly the first specialists to do this, but their doctrine has gained credibility in some very high offices. Why?

This is another "emperor's new clothes" assumption. It is assumed to be true because questioning it, or differing with it, might make even a secure executive (if there is such a thing) seem unsophisticated and foolish. It seems logical that only a simpleminded creature would say that data is bunk. The fact is that information is important, and having it can be advantageous or even necessary to businesses of all sorts, but it just is not the most important factor in business. Money and people are both more important. Another misleading factor is that discussing "data" in the abstract, allowing the term to cover every sort of information, is pure sophistry. But from this illusory basis, it has been easy to overemphasize the importance of the data management aspect of information technology, which even today manages only a fraction of the information used by any business. Many data management groups have influence in their organizations out of all proportion to their potential contribution.

There is a case history associated with this assumption that is perhaps the most tragic example of mismanagement in the sad history of information technology:

A very successful discount retail business located in Florida seemed to be able to do no wrong as it grew across the southern tier of states in the U.S. Its leadership was energetic and enlightened. Unfortunately, they became convinced that the chief information officer's faith in the latest fad in data management—called object-oriented systems—would provide even more growth. As the company invested millions in the OOPS (object-oriented programming system) project, the chief information officer went from trade show to trade show bragging about it. He predicted that systems would be created that would be immediately responsive to all changing business needs. These systems were to be more closely aligned to the business than any built by traditional means. He predicted better control over the company's invaluable data, and more responsive contacts with suppliers and customers. He was wrong. The senior management of the company were also wrong to put a set of completely new systems, built using completely untried methods, on line all at once. The company found that the systems did not work. Orders were not placed, shipments were not sent. Pricing had to be done by hand. Nothing, in fact, worked. The company was ruined almost overnight. It was forced into bankruptcy by the assumption that a data-oriented approach to business had to be the best approach.

Few businesses have been destroyed by their own "data whomper" staff, but many information systems projects have failed due to their key assumption. All of the projects that attempted to bring their companies' data into a single database have failed. There are few information technology specialists who will suggest a single database now, but there are many who espouse somewhat less ambitious data warehouses that are still too complex to succeed. In general, data should pay its way like any other business support tool, and be justified based upon immediate return. Data just isn't a panacea. Any modern business manager, given the choice of having control of all the data in the business, all the people in the business, or all the money in the business, would be well advised to pick the money or the people. Data is not even a close third.

ASSUMPTION 7.9
INFORMATION TECHNOLOGY MANAGEMENT IS JUST A MATTER OF BUYING THE RIGHT HARDWARE AND SOFTWARE.

Many business people feel that information technology needs no real management. They assume that it is possible to simply purchase the right hardware and software for the business, and then sit back and watch the results. They think anyone can do these things. This assumption is becoming more common as personal computer experience makes nontechnical business people think they know all they need to know. Success would be a lot easier if this were true, but it is not.

It is true that anyone can buy hardware. One of the best approaches to buying hardware is to ignore any information about what is available on the market and just present business requirements to the suppliers. This forces the vendors to pick the right hardware and to describe (and even demonstrate) how the hardware will support the business. Competition keeps the prices down. But this is not the end of the story. The hardware must be managed and maintained. Furthermore, there is more than hardware involved in information technology support. Software is much more difficult to buy than hardware.

The other factors supporting information technology use in business are even more complicated than software and equally important. The Sloan School at MIT did an extensive study to identify and quantify the success factors for information technology in business. They found it more complex than expected, and their expectations were not simple. One consistency they were able to measure was that companies that spent as much on technology support elements as on the technology itself were obtaining much better benefits from the technology. The support factors they found were planning for technology implementations, training, maintenance, and hot-line user services, among others. It seems that the majority of businesses surveyed by this study were buying technology and then not incurring enough support expense to use it effectively. This is also what we have seen in our consulting practice. The users of technology themselves contribute to the problem when they ask for variances from company standards to buy, for example, a new spreadsheet program. The assumption is made that such a request comes from one who knows the product wanted and will use it well. In fact, the requesters often just see something advertised, are dazzled by it, fight to buy it, and then spend company time learning to use it on their own.

Even in the area of choosing hardware, which should be straightforward for professional computer technicians, it should not be assumed that just buying something is all that is required. A somewhat amusing example occurred some years ago at the International Monetary Fund (we include the name of this organization because it is in the public sector).

> The Fund bought an attractive solution to its requirement to connect its main building in Washington with some temporary space they were renting in other buildings nearby. The telephone company could not, at the time, connect its Centrex intercom systems across Pennsylvania Avenue. The solution the Fund located was a laser link. When first installed it worked, but the inexperienced staff at the Fund did not know how to keep it working. The link would frequently become misaligned, causing communication to be cut off, sometimes in one direction only. It was not uncommon to place a call and hear a voice saying: "I know you can hear me, but I can't hear you. If you want to complain, call X at the following number ...." Anyone can buy technology, but getting it to work properly is not always so easy.

ASSUMPTION 7.10
THE INFORMATION TECHNOLOGY STAFF (AND ITS
MANAGEMENT) DO NOT UNDERSTAND THE BUSINESS.

Most business people assume that computer technicians do not understand their particular business. Some even say that they do not understand business at all. This assumption is largely true. This assumption should not be challenged by senior management, it should just be recognized and fixed. But can it be fixed? The assumption that underlies this one is that it cannot, and it is this assumption that ought to be challenged.

Most information technology departments are keenly aware of this assumption and have been contending with it for years. It is amazing how much effort has been expended to overcome this insidious assumption. The first attempts began when on-line systems became popular. On-line systems, by the most basic aspect of their nature, moved the computer into operations areas where only printed reports had been before. The systems technicians needed a closer rapport with their users and often created highly specialized positions within their organizations to represent the interests of specific customers. However, the demands of the on-line system were greater than all but a few systems groups could meet. The requirement for response to changing business needs was in fundamental conflict with the technical effort and attention to detail that on-line systems required. User dissatisfaction drove the systems groups further from their users even as they tried to get closer.

Attempts to become more businesslike took many forms over the years since the early 1970s. Technical staff has placed all sorts of criteria on what it meant to understand and be part of the business. They assumed that being businesslike meant being formal in making presentations, learning more of the business' terminology, appearing more professional in the way they managed themselves, and sounding more sophisticated about the industries they worked in. The simplicity of the true disconnection between information technology and business staff has not even yet occurred to most systems technicians. The real meaning of business is profit and the missing links are only these two:

1. The I/T staff cannot predict the impact that a dollar they spend has on the bottom line (either a base dollar or an incremental one).

2. The I/T department has yet to find a way to capture the details of how work is done in the business areas they support. From the oldest (requirements analysis) to the newest (object-oriented programming based on data models), the methods used by I/T cannot show how business' work is being done. They really do not understand the business.

Only when information technology learns to do these two things and do them consistently will business recognize them as colleagues.

The case of an Eastern insurance company is illustrative.

A large insurance company invested in a multimillion-dollar effort to build a new claims system. The requirements analysis was conducted in a perfunctory fashion by two groups: data analysts who charted data relationships so that a database could be defined using a database management system, and systems analysts who defined the requirements in terms of how the new system was to differ from the old one. No one even looked at the way the work was currently being done in detail, no one spent time watching claims being processed, no one tried to analyze the factors that contributed to speed and efficiency, and no one challenged any of the current workflow assumptions related to the processing of claims. The system was built and is now in operation. Its implementation was fought bitterly by some of the operations personnel who process claims. They complained that the new system was slower and less reliable than the old systems. Even when this happened, the systems department did not send representatives to watch the work as it was being done. To this day, the operations staff assumes that the systems staff does not understand the business. And they are absolutely right.

This problem can be solved.

CHALLENGING INFORMATION TECHNOLOGY ASSUMPTIONS

The most misleading assumption to challenge in this area is that the company is doing as well as it can in using information technology. There is *no* company that cannot improve its bottom line by better use of technology. There is an immediate opportunity for most large companies, both the technology advantaged and disadvantaged, to review all their systems. When the year 2000 begins, nearly every old computer system, having reserved only two digits for the year in all date fields, will not process time periods properly. A span of a few weeks from December 1999 to January 2000 will seem to the computer to be a negative 99 years. In other words, the entire world of legacy systems and the businesses that they support will be threatened in a few hundred working days from now. If the usual maintenance is done to correct this problem, it will cost most large companies millions of dollars, and they will get nothing else out of it except possibly even more degradation of their old systems. Smart businesses will use this crisis as an opportunity to change things. The first step is to objectively evaluate what information technology is really supporting, in terms of the business processes. To do this the old myths and assumptions must be cast aside.

SOME PRINCIPLES FOR INFORMATION TECHNOLOGY MANAGEMENT

A few words of guidance for business managers can help them look objectively at information technology:

1. The most important activity in information technology management is protecting data: from loss, from outside attack (hacking), from unauthorized access within the company, from inaccuracy.

2. When users report a problem, there virtually always is a problem. The possibility that they are just doing something wrong or there was a one-time anomaly that will never recur is too re-

mote to be seriously considered. However, the problem is almost never what the users think it is. The roots of information technology problems are complex and deep.

3. It is almost always better to take the time required to do preparatory work in information technology. The usual practice is to assume that since it will take longer to do anything new, it therefore will be better to just do it, but this assumption is a very bad one for technology work. An interesting example occurred in Australia.

A small group of programmers accepted a systems development contract for a 12-month effort that should have been 24 months. Another much larger group had already failed to develop the same system properly. The small group assessed the available technology tools, decided that they needed a better one, and spent 11 of their 12 months developing not the system, but a new fourth-generation language. The new language was so good that they were able to write the system's programs in one month and to deliver it on contracted schedule. Burroughs (now Unisys) adopted the new language as a key development tool for its computers.

There are many such cases, all leading to the conclusion that taking the time to do something right improves not only quality, but efficiency in the computer field.

4. The only place to justify technology is at the bottom line. The difference in the bottom line between using some proposed technology and not using it is its benefit. Time savings, responsiveness, and other local measurements are not reliable.

5. Managers of operations staff who use computers have been told for years that they need to become computer literate. Though they have been harried for years to do it, knowing the internal functions of a computer will not help user managers at all. Even knowing how to program computers can only add to the problem by giving managers the completely false idea that they know everything necessary about information technology. Programming or knowing how to operate a personal computer no more prepares a manager for information technology in business than knowing how to read prepares any layperson to practice law. What is needed is better called computer management literacy, the specific knowledge of how to manage I/T for business. The areas that should be learned are:

- information technology capabilities
- information technology limitations
- information technology methodologies
- information technology costs.

This information is not readily available, but any business should be able to develop an in-house course that covers all of them, for the technologies and methods that the company uses.

EVOLUTIVE TECHNOLOGY DEPLOYMENT

A reasonable question to ask when it is obvious that both extremes and compromises have failed, as they have for information technology in business, is: "Is there a better way?" There is, and it is called Evolutive Technology Deployment (ETD). Evolutive is the same term described in Chapter 2: not evolutionary, which implies passivity and slowness, but instead a controlled process of focused, high-business-impact changes, each of which is made very rapidly.

Deployment is a departure from development. It means to establish technology support for a business operation (a part of a business process) using an appropriate combination of methods, computers, business rules, communications, computer programs (bought or built, new and old), data, and human resources (people, procedures, policies, training). Deployment is much broader than development in that it includes technology components other than newly-written computer code, and also in that it takes into account all of the components that affect how the work is done, not just the business requirements, computer programs, and data that were the concerns of systems development. This new approach is recommended for three reasons:

1. The old approaches do not work. In fact, they never worked— they took too long, cost too much, and virtually never satisfied the business needs that motivated them. Few systems have been maintainable or modifiable. The results have been so poor that the rate of new systems development has slowed to a trickle compared with the flood of 15 years ago.

2. The new end user technologies require a new basic approach. Their general-purpose capabilities must be used cooperatively with the central mainframe capabilities and the data stored on them.

3. Implementing a new system by old systems development methods usually ignores the existence of current systems that must be interfaced with the new ones so that the work of both new and old systems can go forward. Many new systems development efforts have been turned into a hopelessly complex morass when interfacing them with the old systems was attempted. Alternatives to interfacing have usually required the business to be run very inefficiently for protracted periods while old technologies are phased into newer ones. This problem also affects the design of new support: alternatives are limited to either living with old systems or replacing them at very high costs. The hybrid system, which would seem to be the most cost-effective solution, has been proposed, but it usually fails because it cannot be built using current methods.

ETD solves these problems. Its most important component is speed. The term " evolutive " was coined partly to show that, unlike evolution, ETD is immediately effective in dealing with each small, contained increment of change. No approach will be of benefit to business if it is not immediate. Rapid is not fast enough. ETD is also a natural extension of what is being done, using an overall framework to supply common design capabilities, focus, and control for all of the diverse components that are inescapably intertwined in the technology support of business today.

THE COMPONENTS OF BUSINESS OPERATIONS

The components of business operations that are addressed by computer systems have been established as process and data for some time. Data has been represented by Peter Chen's entity relationship diagrams (ERD) for over twenty years with some satisfactory results. This definition of data has two problems, however. First, ERDs do not have any time or movement sense. They show only the static relationships between data entities, and thus require that entities be defined. This is somewhat restrictive. Data changes as it moves through a business process. The ERD also covered less definition than needed: it defined only a limited scope of business objects. The modern approach is to define data "objects," which then become reusable building blocks for systems. Object-oriented coding is the latest fad, but it seems to be a useful one in that greater speed and lower price are certainly facilitated.

Process, on the other hand, has never been acceptably defined. The current interest in reengineering provides the basis for some solutions in technology: we can now describe the process of a business and the process performed by a system in the same basic language. However, one more advance is needed, as was the case for data: the basic unit, or building block, must be identified if immediate deployment is to be achieved. The basic unit defined by Evolutive Technology Deployment is the "episode of interaction," or EOI. *An EOI is a series of actions that relate a business process to a set of data objects.* An EOI can also relate a set of objects to another, as is the case in a data conversion or the preparation of a printed report. The EOI, once defined, is immediately translatable into a reusable module of computer code, or pseudo-code, that can be compiled and then run on a variety of platforms (this depends upon the code itself, of course). An EOI can also be translated into a procedure to be followed by a person, an algorithm or mathematical formula, a set of macro instructions for a spreadsheet—indeed, anything procedural or any decision-making rule.

So, the basic (very basic) approach of ETD is to develop data object definitions and EOIs that will supply about 80 to 90 percent of a new technology system, and then put them together to form the system. Some technology vendors are now predefining data objects for business, so even that job will be speeded up in the near future. The EOIs can be generated by code generation technology. The next issue is to determine how these building blocks should be put together. How is the architecture of the business and its systems to be designed?

The design is started by mapping the current business operation. This should include all of the dimensions of the operation, not just process and data. The whole picture forms a business architecture or framework.

The key elements of the current business map and the new design are:

• mapping business activity or workflow, step by step;
• discovering business rules as they govern activity;
• discovering human resource elements;
• factoring in the vision, plans, and objectives of the company;
• mapping the relationships between the process, the technology, the data, the human resources, the business plans, and the business rules; and
• gathering quantitative data for the current performance of the operation.

MODELING THE BUSINESS OPERATION— THE NEW DESIGN APPROACH

When the map of the current business operation is complete, the new one can be designed using simulation. Simulation should help to predict the best solution to the problem, and will also provide the first cut of the new system design.

TESTING

Testing is an essential part of the development process, but is often forgotten or given insufficient attention. Old methods of systems testing, especially for mixed systems such as client/server systems, can be very difficult. ETD provides its own testing tool: the system is testing itself against its design.

MAINTENANCE

ETD systems are maintained at the design level. This means that instead of looking for hours or days into program listings, the maintenance technicians look at design documents, make changes in them, and regenerate the program code. The effort is cut by 50 to 75 percent, which removes the backlog problem and, at last, makes the company's computer systems responsive to its business needs.

THE FUTURE OF TECHNOLOGY

Technology is certain to improve in the future. Many of the improvements that are forecast apply to making technology easy to use. Until that goal is achieved, however, it is using technology that is the essential challenge to the business person. Technology today can cost more to use than it saves. Managers should test their assumptions about technology every time a computer decision is required.

JUST DON'T RELY UPON CONSENSUS

BUSINESSES ARE PLAGUED BY INDECISION.

Consensus management is becoming increasingly common in business. It has not received as much attention as some of business's other recent changes, but it is amazingly widespread. All things considered, it is not a good change. Instead of improving the quality of decision making, consensus management appears to be increasing indecision, which is never good in business. Would a football team win that allowed the players to decide each play by vote? A team run this way would probably not only lose, it would not be able to get off a single play within the allotted time. Then why would a business follow such an approach?

The reasons for the rise in consensus management in business are complex. Whether from fear, inflexibility, or a business structure that fails to promote responsibility, too many companies are unable or unwilling to make decisions. Many companies are virtually frozen in place. In many cases the operation is effectively leaderless, as its managers spend all their time in meetings that resolve little.

Some American businesses have evolved into semisocial meeting clubs. Managers and staff members spend a significant portion of their time, often over half of the average ten hours per day that management works, in meetings. Many managers' schedules are completely filled with meetings; they leave some meetings early to get to others late. Overscheduling is a must and a problem for some managers. The telltale symptom of this problem is seen when scheduling any meeting or work requires weeks or months of advance notice.

A frightful example of how far this conflict can go occurred at a large hospital on the west side of Chicago.

> A Chicago teaching hospital was unable to improve its administrative processes. One of the roadblocks was commonly thought to be the number of meetings that were taking place. No one had time for anything else. To remedy this situation, the administrative group required that all meetings be scheduled two months in advance. But this edict did not consider the need for schedule changes. Conflicts in scheduling invariably occurred during the two months spent waiting for each meeting, and schedules had to be changed. Virtually every meeting was changed at least once. The average was about three changes per scheduled meeting. All of the hospital's meetings thus took about six months to schedule and take place.

The question in this type of business environment is: how can anything ever get done? Just accomplishing anything or finishing anything in this environment is impossible. Change is faster than any response that is possible under this type of operating environment and the company cannot hold its own.

THE NEED FOR CONSENSUS

The driving force behind the explosion in meetings was the acceptance of a need for consensus on issues. Initially this approach was very good and worthwhile. It was applied to serious problems and complex issues. It was a type of management teaming that provided multiple views. The problem is that companies now have too much of a good thing. No one seems to be able to do anything alone today and the need for group consensus has filtered down to all levels in the company and to even minor decisions or changes.

The drive toward consensus management was based on two underlying assumptions:

1. If everyone agrees, there is a better chance of being right.
2. Consensus means that everyone will support the work.

Both assumptions have been proven to be wrong.

One of the sources of the current consensus trend is the credibility that participative management gained from the Japanese management model. U.S. managers discovered the Japanese reliance upon consensus management at a time when many Japanese business practices were being emulated in the U.S. and around the world. Japanese business people had come from nowhere to become the world's business giants. They were taking over markets and virtually crushing their competition. As a result, consensus management was widely accepted.

However, as William G. Ouchi pointed out in his seminal work on applying Japanese methods to American business, *Theory Z,* the Japanese model was not fully understood, much less emulated. In Japan, consensus was an extension of Japanese social culture, and was carried on in a ritual, called *Ringi.* Japanese business did not use the mechanism of large meetings to obtain consensus, but assigned a small (usually three-member) committee to obtain consensus (and formal signatures) from every manager who would be affected by the proposed change. The managers interviewed by the committee could ask for changes in the proposal, but there was really no way to simply object to it or to forestall it. Whatever time was lost in *Ringi* was made up in implementing the proposal after it was approved. In American business, none of these features were ever used, and participative management continued to be ineffective. Ouchi cited unfavorable experiences in U.S. consensus management going back as far as 1969.

We are certainly not the better for consensus management today. The problem is not with the concept, but with the way it has evolved and been applied in American business.

Clearly a team has a potential for making a better decision than an individual. However, there are many requisites to effective team management. For example, the team must be dedicated to making that decision as quickly as possible. There is no question that speed is the exception in actual practice. Consensus is now an excuse for doing nothing in many companies. It is strangling these companies.

Consensus has become the easy way to say no. No one can be fully to blame in this approach, so no one can be punished if something doesn't work out. Because no one is accountable, everyone gains a type of anonymity and immunity to reprisals. In these companies, when the team must make tough calls, they bring in a puppet consulting firm who will agree with them, but shield them: the company can blame them if things go awry.

But consensus can be useful in certain activities. It is desirable in design decisions. It is important in coordinating production changes. It is even good in planning. It is not good in daily decision making or in choosing a course of action from among several alternatives.

THE CONSENSUS MEETING DILEMMA

Operational meetings in many companies are based on reaching a consensus—eventually. In these companies it seems important for managers to be team players. It is also important for them to be participants in as many things as possible—not only is it good to be seen as being involved, but something might work and they might get points.

Managers and staff members in these companies must prove continuously that they can compromise and reach a consensus with their peers. So consensus building is practiced. It becomes a game and a culture and it becomes a way to avoid conflict and risk. Everyone involved usually knows how the game works and how they should play it. If anyone becomes too aggressive or too much of a threat to the status quo, that person is branded as a troublemaker, loner, and rogue. These people are ostracized and their careers suffer.

The dilemma is thus one of complacency and never rocking the boat as opposed to accomplishing tasks. The other downside of the problem is the need to attend a nonstop series of meetings.

A computer systems steering committee in a large firm boasted about twenty members. These people all believed that they needed to be involved (to promote their personal interests) in projects that affected them and their operations. In fact, if any member was absent from a meeting, work for their area was skipped and delayed at least a week.

Because no meeting was attended by all twenty people, decisions for many systems could not be made. Meeting minutes were written and passed out before the next meeting, but the participants were always too busy to read them before the meetings. As a result, every meeting began with at least an hour's rehashing of the last meeting to bring the absent managers up to speed on new problems and actions. The debates often changed priorities as stronger managers pushed their interests more successfully than weaker ones. The result was a constant state of review and a continuing shifting of priority. Out of any meeting at least three-fourths of the time was spent on the past. Often there was too little time to address the current requests. This shifting and reworking caused a serious lack of focus so that many efforts were started and then lost in the priority shuffle. Little was accomplished, but a lot of time was spent doing it.

PROCRASTINATION AND STAGNATION

In some companies the culture seems to encourage procrastination: never, never do today what you can put off until tomorrow. Projects that are approved never seem to get started. If meetings produce results, this is a bonus. But if they do not result in positive deliverables, are they really worthwhile? As an example, a sales group was oriented toward "taking the next step." They were very good at this. They always set up another session at the conclusion of the current one. They always had a next step and their managers loved them. However, while they always had a prospective client to talk to, they never managed to close sales. The sales cycle just went on and on. While there was a lot of hard work, there were no deliverables.

While no one should force someone to do something they are not ready to do, it is also important to note when something is really stagnating and when the people you are interacting with are really procrastinating. Many companies are quite good at forcing stagnation. They put up roadblocks everywhere. They have good excuses. They accomplish their personal goal: everything just stands still in spite of the amount of time, effort, and resources spent.

AVOIDING RISK AT ALMOST ALL COST

We have all heard of risk aversion. Many managers believe it is good to be risk-averse and to let everyone know it. When applied to a person or a given operation, this term is synonymous with procrastination. It is not just a way of assessing risk and then limiting exposure. It is rather an aversion to exposure. These managers avoid change and they avoid anything that is new or potentially visible. They are often the ones who wait until a project is clearly succeeding and then claim ownership.

> At a large processing company, a project was undertaken to correct a serious operational problem. The project had been launched three times before and had failed each time. The fourth try was considered high-risk and a waste of time by most managers. This time the project was given to a new officer. No one else wanted to touch the effort. After about two months, the project was clearly a success. It was succeeding through the use of a new approach. When the success of the effort was insured, a higher-level manager became energized and justified moving the project from the new officer to himself. Because this senior manager had been marginally associated with the project, he took full credit for the success. The new officer was not happy, but was not able to do anything about the situation.

AVOIDING CONTROVERSY

Astute managers have learned that progression through certain types of corporate ranks depends on avoiding unnecessary controversy. In some companies, just surviving requires that all controversy and contention be avoided. Controversial issues and the teams that are formed to address them are often avoided; everyone disappears when volunteers are sought. The fact is that controversial issues are the ones that often carry the highest impact on the business. The risk is not for the faint of heart. In fact, according to many managers it is for the fools in the organization. The approach to avoiding controversy is often to form a committee of ten to twenty people. This group is large enough to spread the risk and find someone who will accept responsibility for the committee. Because it is almost impossible to get twenty people together, meetings seldom occur. When they do, people are missing and of course a decision cannot be made without including everyone. And so on ...

ASSUMPTION 8.1
A DECISION REACHED BY A GROUP IS BETTER THAN ONE REACHED BY AN INDIVIDUAL.

No one knows everything about everything. No one is competent in all areas. Everyone has strengths and weaknesses and everyone has a different background and a different perspective. Consensus building is an attempt to recognize these truths and to mitigate the weaknesses of some through the strengths of others. Practice and theory, however, can be two different things and in this case, they are.

The original concept is that a team of people with diverse but applicable backgrounds would work together on a given or common problem to create a composite approach that would be built upon the strengths that each member could bring to bear. In a perfect business environment this might even work. In the world of modern business, this concept becomes flawed by the realities of human nature and corporate politics.

First of all, teams are not always staffed by people with appropriate backgrounds. They are not always staffed by people who have the authority to make decisions and they are not staffed by people who have anything to gain by the success of the project. Participants often bring a lot of baggage to the table. There are old animosities, rivalries, and distrusts. There are personal agendas and personal definitions and personal loyalties and personal obligations.

Given all this, a decision that is reached by many is still better than one reached by a single person. But where do you draw the line? The deck can be stacked for or against a project by the person selecting the team. Furthermore, as the team members are usually individually selected by managers in the areas that are affected, any manager can skew the team's views and recommendations. When skewing in an opposing direction happens as a result of other participants' agendas, a battle starts. The debating begins as individual managers' opinions are backed and alliances are made. While this is reality, it is also clearly unproductive.

To show good faith, many consensus-oriented companies believe that they must get everyone who may be affected involved in the decision process. The teams in these companies are usually large. After all, if a team makes a better decision than an individual, a big group must be able to make better choices than a small group. And if the group is big, the size alone protects everyone from blame.

In a medium-sized Midwest manufacturing company, a team of managers assigned to review the recommendations of an expensive study became deadlocked over one issue. Try as they might, they were evenly split on a key decision. Their managers next got involved; they represented their personal interests and no one would give in. Finally, they elected to make no decision. This default decision to do nothing caused the study to be canceled and the great benefits of the effort to be lost.

This example also points out that the assumption of willingness to compromise is often questionable. Unless the corporate culture insists on compromise, any disagreement can stop a project.

At a large Chicago-area medical center a key manager was involved in many projects. To promote acceptance and commitment, the hospital insisted that a consensus approach be used in all projects. The teams were made of representatives from most of the business, clinical, and technical groups of the hospital. The information technology representative won a nickname that he was very proud of: "Doctor No." This name represented his stand on most issues that had any systems requirement. Was this loyalty to the information services department? Arguably, yes. They had limited resources. Was this in the best interest of the hospital? Clearly, no. In this case, the committees were ruled by a strong player—in a noncritical area.

ASSUMPTION 8.2
IN A CONSENSUS ENVIRONMENT, EVERYONE WILL NATURALLY WORK FOR THE COMMON GOOD OF THE COMPANY.

Unfortunately, personal interests will not be overcome for the best decision or for the good of the company. No one wants to be the one who is cut or the one who gets more work from a change. Corporate interests naturally take a back seat to personal concerns. This assumption is thus accurate only when the people involved perceive an advantage. It is thus advantageous to create win–win situations. But most of the time, someone loses. The loser and any allies can be expected to create roadblocks to progress.

This situation does not change with the number of people participating in the decision or activity. A common belief is that politics and self-interest will be overwhelmed if a large enough group is involved. Experience shows that this is not true. The greater the number of participants, the greater the chance of disruption and failure. More is not always better. In fact the greater the number of participants, the greater the problem of reaching a consensus on anything (even where to go to lunch).

An example of this is in approving a document that formalizes what everyone on a team has agreed upon. Each person will change it a little. Some will beat the wording to death. Some will focus on an obscure point and some will camouflage their true intent to change it to their personal advantage. The agreed-upon document will require several rewrites as comments are included and then re-reviewed. After all, "It is important that we get this exactly right so there will be no misunderstanding." Unfortunately, with the hidden nuances and new vocabulary that will creep into the document, the meaning will always be open to debate.

In addition to the endless disagreement that most consensus-oriented teams must endure, compromise almost always dilutes the point being made until it is too generalized to promote the real intent of the issue. No hard-line policies are made and no definitive actions are taken. Middle-of-the-road everything is not in the best interest of the company. This approach has clearly failed in politics and it is failing in business.

Because people cannot be expected to put the company first on their own initiative, the definition of what is in the best interest of the company must be agreed upon by senior management and then clearly articulated to the upper and mid-level managers. These managers must then be monitored to make certain that the best interest of the company is foremost in all efforts. Today, this definition does not take place because management assumes it is in the personal best interest of everyone to see the company succeed. While this may have been true years ago, there are enough examples to prove that it is often not true today. Staff mobility and downsizing have destroyed loyalty; and this lack of a corporate perspective is one of the results.

A mid-sized supply firm was unhappy with its information technology support. The operations managers felt that they were not being adequately supported. The backlog of requests was over a thousand and the list was getting longer. There was no way the information technology group could keep up. A prioritization team of over twenty members was formed to give direction to the information technology group. Each member represented personal interests and infighting became the principal activity. As a result, no real priorities were set and nothing was really agreed upon. Members missed meetings and when they came, many of them were not prepared. Re-review and revision of decisions slowed everything down further. The only people who were happy about the group's lack of progress were the information technology group: they got a break as the work backlogged in the prioritization group.

ASSUMPTION 8.3
WORK GROUPS WERE CREATED TO SOLVE PROBLEMS AND IMPROVE QUALITY; THE GROUP MEMBERS MUST WORK THINGS OUT AMONG THEMSELVES.

Self-directed, high-performance teams can and should manage themselves. This assumption is valid in some cases. Unfortunately, it is invalid in many others. Teams are not universal solutions to all management problems.

The concept of self-directed teams removes the team from direct manager authority. It flattens the operation, but it also forces the team members to be confrontational with one another. In theory, anyone who is not pulling his or her weight will be pressured by the other team members into doing a good job. If the right people are involved, this works. When unproductive employees are put on a work team, they continue to do what they always have done: try to get away with doing as little work as possible. The team members have no real authority over them. They can argue, but they cannot force an issue or take personnel actions.

As negative personalities spoil the process and the glue of cooperation melts, the team will begin to disintegrate. Peer pressure becomes a dead issue as relationships fall apart. When animosity or competition for the jobs on the team begin, the team members often begin to drift apart. Peer pressure is viewed as cliquish or clannish and the team may begin to re-form into new cliques for support.

As the teams evolve and form alliances into subgroups, group members often lose a team perspective. Thus, although many team members wish to do their part and implement their changes according to the wishes of the team, the team falls into the almost unavoidable trap of all consensus groups—endless squabbling and procrastination.

Another erroneous assumption is that everyone on the team will live up to their stated commitments to the team and provide the time and resources needed. Experience shows that this is generally a false assumption. Many team members are part-time members. Many teams are only part-time teams. All members are expected to get their "full-time" or "day" jobs done in addition to their team responsibilities. The meeting and ongoing work requirements alone cause conflicts. In addition to these conflicts are the priority conflicts: other things are more important. The results are missed meetings and a lack of time to prepare for those meetings that are attended.

As decisions are made without team members being present, the products can be skewed to provide advantage to specific departments or people. As this happens, the team will begin to quarrel and lose focus. Without a central team leader who has authority, the team will fail.

Assumption 8.4
Making no decision is better than making the wrong decision.

Fear of rejection, scorn, and reprisal has caused this assumption to be valid in some companies. Although it would seem that only a few managers would consciously accept this assumption, there are certainly many managers whose business lives are unconsciously ruled by it. The assumption hides in many closely-related guises that are only occasionally voiced by insecure managers.

A typical excuse is, "This is an important decision; we cannot afford to get it wrong." Another is, "It is better to spend time and money up front than to back away from a bad decision." Unfortunately, no decision is a decision. The problem is that it freezes any progress. The real issue is the question, "Why can't a decision be made?"

In many projects, highly beneficial activities have been put on indefinite hold as the managers agonized over a decision. In many cases, the budget was approved, the project teams had a recommendation, and all the studies were completed. Still the managers procrastinated. Often the excuse is that there are too many more important things going on right now to start something new.

Teams can have similar problems. It is very easy for a whole team to refuse to make decisions. They often say that the decision is up to senior managers and they themselves are not being given proper guidance. This is actually a cultural issue, rather than a structural one. The teams are uncomfortable making a decision so they present a problem to their managers and hope they will get an answer. This approach is often used in politically sensitive areas or for decisions that the team considers high-risk. The managers don't want to deal with the problem; that is the team's job. The managers want to approve recommended solutions and they want the team to implement the solution they approve. This disconnection is common and represents a real threat to a rapid response to opportunity.

Procrastination in decision making, starting a project, or implementing a directive, while common, is a real roadblock to success. The decision, project, or implementation is needed for a specific reason. As long as the nondecision puts off the benefit that will be provided by the action, the company loses.

CHALLENGING ASSUMPTIONS ABOUT CONSENSUS MANAGEMENT

The ability to recognize the effect of a company's internal culture and the way the company really functions is the first step in controlling management decision making. Controlling decision making is the foundation of success in controlling change. The consensus approach has been used for many years and is an ingrained part of many corporate cultures. While it is often misused and creates its own problems, the concept is good. The issue then is how to fix the problems with this approach.

The truthful answer is that the issues and assumptions discussed in this chapter are very common. They exist in every operation. But they can be overcome.

IMPROVING THE CONSENSUS PROCESS: THE FORCED CONSENSUS APPROACH

A variation on consensus management that has proven to provide the benefits but not the drawbacks is "Forced Consensus." Forced consensus is based on the belief that a team manager must drive the team to a decision. The objective of the consensus approach should be defined as a sharing of ideas and backgrounds. Consensus should be redefined as a majority vote, not 100 percent agreement. The consensus team must have a manger who is empowered to make decisions on procedure and force a vote. All members must accept the outcome.

The team is responsible for raising issues and obtaining valid information. Every piece of information should be questioned and answers required. No one can be allowed to hide information. The team must share this information and raise additional significant questions. Smoke screen questions must be avoided and the team manager must stop them. Any issue that is obviously a personal agenda item must also be stopped. In the final analysis, the team must be able to vote on what they will talk about and consider. If the team manager believes that no progress is being made or that personal agenda items are being raised, he or she must call for a vote from the team on topics that will be addressed. Of course, an assumption will be made that the topic is not appropriate if the team chooses to delete it and the meeting minutes will reflect the vote and the assumption. Pleasing everybody is not important; focus and objectivity are.

Any discussion must also have time limits. Each person should be given a specific amount of time to present an opinion. Presentations should, of course, receive more time. At the end of the allotted discussion and debate time, a vote is mandatory.

Every topic and issue will be brought to the full team after the information has been obtained and analyzed by a subteam. After a preset discussion, the manager must force a vote. There are three possible results: yes, no, or need additional information. The third category cannot be allowed to be general. Only specific information needs are acceptable. If additional information is needed, a subteam will be assigned the task and a schedule will be agreed upon. The issue will again come to the full committee for a vote at the scheduled time. If more information is needed again, the full team must set up a workshop and complete the issue at that time. Fortunately, this option is virtually never necessary.

Once voted on, the issue is finalized. It will not be allowed to be changed unless new data is found or related business activities or rules change. If appropriate, the issue will again flow through the above process.

In the event of a deadlock, a higher authority is called. This manager has the authority to break the deadlock and cast a vote to decide the issue.

While this is not a pure consensus, the Forced Consensus approach supports a multi-person view, an open discussion, the definition and analysis of appropriate information, and the belief that multiple perspectives provide the best answer. It doesn't, however, allow endless discussion and fussing over trivia. It also tends to lessen the impact of personal agendas. Everyone has a chance to speak his or her mind and then there is a vote, with no filibusters and no procrastination.

JUST DON'T ALLOW INDECISION

In many companies a significant amount of time is spent avoiding making decisions. Procrastination is hidden behind such euphemisms as "due diligence" and "we must prove the numbers." The fear of making a wrong decision has resulted in widespread shirking of decision making. Even simple decisions often take months of meetings and analysis. Consensus is, of course, needed in any decision, so teams are set up and money is spent. Cycle time and staff time are wasted.

In several companies more is spent on the decision process than was spent on a purchase. When financial or procedural controls create a burden on the consensus team and the operation, they should be changed. When they allow or promote procrastination, they should be eliminated. When the red tape slows things down, it should be cut. While these precepts are easy to write, entrenched practice and policy are difficult to even review, let alone change. Too many people have too much of a vested interest. However, any progress that can be made in controlling these activities will provide immediate and potentially significant benefits.

Decisions are why managers are needed. When this role has been changed, it should be reviewed and redirected to allow managers to perform their real activities. This part of a manager's job cannot be suspended through membership on a team that must reach consensus. Membership on a consensus team or forming a team cannot take managers off the hook. The decision is still their responsibility.

Consider reviewing who should be making decisions. Ask what those decisions address and what authority the manager or staff member has in making the decision. Look into needed decision cycles—optimum decision time frames and actual decision time frames. Define the impact of the potential decisions and tie everything together. Then review the decision process and flow. This is the basis for a decision management matrix.

PROCRASTINATION—NEVER DO TODAY WHAT CAN BE PUT OFF

Some managers and workers are experts at procrastination. They follow the drawer escalation theory: start by putting any request in the bottom drawer. Each time someone asks about the request, move it up a drawer. When it reaches the top of your desk, pay attention to it. Until then, procrastinate. Make excuses. After all, the overburdened and understaffed excuse has worked in the past. Or be inventive. Excuses work.

> At a large east coast company, a senior manager was responsible for 1,300 people. The manager's supervisor asked that certain changes be evaluated and implemented. The changes had been defined and the new operation designed. What was left was a set of specific studies to test the new design assumptions. The senior manager responded consistently that she could not find the time or staff to do the tests. Because her supervisor was weak and had a tendency to hide in the corporate white space and avoid trouble, nothing was done. Procrastination was part of the corporate culture. Today, with new management, this company has still not evaluated any changes; instead, it is about to reduce staff by 500 people. They are following the financial approach. They have no idea how many people they need, but they do know that they need to cut costs. Procrastination still continues in this firm as decisions are deferred and projects languish without a sponsor—even after they are budgeted.

The only answer to procrastination is direct intervention. Work must be prioritized, scheduled, and performed. Deliverables must be completed on time and within budgets. This requires that management commit itself to monitoring schedules and intervening when they slip.

> A large New England company was in the midst of a serious migration of its computer systems. The migration was a multiyear effort. Improvements to keep the current systems running in the interim were considered necessary given the duration of the migration. The information services department had a backlog of over 1,200 system problems and enhancements. Many of these problems resulted in erroneous financial transactions. A committee of high-level business managers was formed to address this problem. The information services response was to state that they had too much work to do and that they could not rank or schedule these projects. They would get to them when they had the time. The committee met week after week. Nothing happened. The information services mid-level managers were allowed to get away with this refusal to work with the committee and to commit themselves to any schedules.

ENCOURAGING HONEST RESPONSE

One of the keys to avoiding unproductive behavior when consensus is required is to encourage honest opinions in place of defensive reactions. This will not be easy. Culture is probably the most durable characteristic of any company. It either promotes fear or protects against it. Many say that it is a direct reflection of senior management. If they act in a certain way, it will be picked up and promulgated downward through the management ranks to the lowest end of the chain—the worker.

The hardest part of changing culture is getting people to admit that they need to change. The fact that managers have reached a level of personal success suggests that they are doing something right. The problem is that in a negative culture, they are doing all the wrong things right.

Fear often rules the company. When fear is part of the company culture, creativity and the ability to make decisions are seldom found. These key components of a successful company must be built. The consensus approach is a way to create anonymity. When used improperly, fear still rules and nothing much improves. It is thus important to provide any consensus team with the authority, anonymity, and protection needed to get the job done. When this happens, the probability of success greatly improves.

PROMOTING PERSONAL CREATIVITY

Education, not retribution, is the key to creativity. Our basic culture in the U.S. and in most of the world is geared toward getting even or meting out punishment. It is not oriented toward learning from our mistakes. In most operations the question "How could we have avoided this or how can we improve this next time?" is seldom asked at all. But a learning environment should drive the entire change process and the teams that are involved in it.

Growth requires creativity. This requires confidence in the system, the team, and management. When fear is eliminated or at least controlled, creativity can take root.

EMPOWERMENT AND CONSENSUS

The key concept for engaging staff in change is empowerment. It is really meant to address the distribution of authority to make decisions lower in the middle or line management levels and into the senior working levels. There are many problems in achieving empowerment, however. For example, few of those who ought to be empowered are accustomed to making decisions. It also seems that most companies prematurely consider empowered staff's decision capability and decision results in performance evaluations, posing an immediate threat. The result is that empowered people often create a new layer of politically-oriented red tape by following a consensus form of responsibility avoidance. The first thing many empowered people do is form committees and hold meetings on making even simple decisions. The excuse is that everyone needs guidelines and they want "buy-in" from everyone, so everyone needs to be involved. The result is that although a layer of mid-level managers may be eliminated, the newly empowered continue to operate as their bosses did, and nothing is improved.

COST VS. VALUE

IT IS TRUE COST IS THE USUAL CRITERION FOR BUSINESS DECISION MAKING, BUT VALUE IS A BETTER GUIDE.

The first questions in determining a company's future marketing direction are obviously: "What markets should we be in now?" and "What markets should we be moving into in the future?" Where is the greatest opportunity for our particular capabilities? What are the real strengths that we have as a company, and where can we use these strengths to our best advantage?

There are three basic stages in the life cycle of a market: nascent, adolescent, and mature. A company must clearly be concerned with where its own target markets fit. What are the viability and longevity of the current products? The stage of the markets and the product fit for those markets should be key considerations.

Competition is becoming more fierce than at any time in the past—in the global market, more companies than ever before are vying for the same customer bases. Markets are becoming saturated as they mature. Market shares that were virtually guaranteed are now eroding. The financial response has been to cut costs to control the price that the company will charge for the product.

THE MISSING LINKS

Some small minority of businesses have developed effective links among their product development departments, their production departments, and their marketing groups. Operating separately, each makes assumptions about what the others are doing, and about what their own roles should be. Marketing usually gives little priority to small improvements in products (or services) and quality control. The development area feels it is forced to make some assumptions, usually based upon current performance, about what production can do and what the costs of production will be. Production concentrates on cost control, and, hopefully, quality, but does not know what the impact of quality changes might be in many cases.

Cost cutting is the most visible reaction to market pressures in most business' production areas. The initial result of the move to cut costs was massive reductions in force. This resulted in a plethora of negatives that we have talked about in earlier chapters. It also provided a negative impact on quality. However, quality has often been considered to be secondary to price and cost.

Unfortunately, the cost-cutting approach of many companies puts them into a downward spiral of cost versus profit. As the price that can be charged falls, the profits shrink. The financial answer, cut costs, is a natural response. But cost cutting can only go so far. Sooner or later, you will no longer be able to reduce costs. Then what?

While we agree that the short-term solution is based on cost reduction, we challenge all managers to think in a different context. Challenge your paradigms and attitudes.

THE EFFECT OF VALUE ON STRATEGY AND PLANNING

Strategy is once again a key concern for companies. The strategies of downsizing to cut costs and quality improvement have been tried and found to provide some improvement, but the quest for the right answer continues. To this end, companies are once again turning to strategy and planning to guide them through the troubled waters of the coming years.

Another realization is the fact that any strategy will change before it is completely implemented. The market and technology are changing too fast to accept any strategy as firm. So flexibility is the key. What drives this flexibility? Clearly there are a great number of factors—including a total unknown, opportunity. Competition and the market create opportunities and obstacles constantly. The time cycle is not the months or years it once was. It is now almost daily. Companies must be constantly vigilant and they must be able to evaluate and react fast. One of the tools in creating this flexibility and speed is Value Based Evaluation. This approach to determining market potential and product fit is presented later in this chapter. Briefly, value based evaluation is a way to understand the values of the buyers as they relate to products and opportunities. Through this understanding, markets can be redefined and products can be made to fit the buyers in these markets.

As companies move into the future, it is important to understand the key drivers for their markets and the buyer values that must be met in order to succeed. Because these values differentiate products and markets, they become as important or more important than cost or price. Value in this context is different from the value-added concept of the past. In this context, value refers to the qualities of a service or product that make people want it. This is also a different type of value from those obtained through focus groups. It is an understanding of the customer and the market and what drives both. Once understood, it provides flexibility and it provides a different way to look at products and at the market.

ASSUMPTION 9.1

DECREASING THE PRICE ALWAYS INCREASES THE VALUE OF ALL PRODUCTS AND ALL SERVICES TO ALL BUYERS.

The driving force behind change since about 1990 has been the belief that cost must be cut so price can be cut. Stock analysts and investors have given this approach validity by rallying to companies that have undertaken efforts to cut costs, especially downsizing. But the underlying assumption that costs drive prices and prices drive the customers to buy may well be false.

Consider the fact that all products in a given group perform the same basic function. An example is blue jeans. One can find blue jeans for $10 a pair. They do the job and they are inexpensive. Designer jeans retail for over $50 a pair. They do the job, but they are expensive. Arguably, the quality of the designer blue jeans is better, but kids tear holes in both expensive and inexpensive blue jeans. The difference is not in real value or in price. It is in the buyer's perception of value. This is the value that buyers place on a specific product. This value is obviously the most useful basis for product differentiation. It is clearly more of a sales driver than any other marketing factor.

This is not an isolated example. Consider any product: soap, for another example. Again, they all do the job. There is a wide range of prices, among other forms of differentiation. As a buyer's values are considered, the desirability of the product can be manipulated. The same product with small changes can be made to stand apart from the competition. This differentiation has nothing to do with cost. For this example we purposely chose a saturated, mature product in soap. There are a hundred different types of soap. The differentiation is on perceived buyer value. Some have body lotion and some are scented. Some fight bacteria and some provide deodorant protection. Any combination is available. There are designer soaps and medicated soaps and specialty soaps. Each new additive created a new market and, based on perceived value, each was able to tie into a new group of buyers. Price has clearly not been an issue until many competitors have entered the very same submarket. They create a cost pressure that can again be beaten through another change to the product. This creates a new niche or submarket. In some cases it creates a different market.

The fact is that every product market that is profitable will eventually become price sensitive as competing products enter it. As we have seen, any product can become revitalized and differentiated if the company understands what motivates the buyer and then manipulates these values. When this occurs, cost is only an issue in defining the minimum sales price. It is not the issue in defining the price that the product can be sold at. The clear driver here is perceived buyer value. Within limits, the pricing can be targeted to specific socioeconomic groups.

Given these facts, is cost or pricing really the issue, or is it creativity and customer understanding? In many companies that are financially driven, the belief persists that the only driver of any real importance is cost and thus price. We believe that this assumption must be challenged as the starting point in the redefinition of product and market and the identification of the strategy needed to move into these markets.

Assumption 9.2
Value is not a strong product differentiator.

Again, in many companies the concept of buyer value is either nonexistent or confined to marketing. Many companies focus on internally perceived need. They say to themselves: "People need to do something, and they need our product to do it." They even go so far as to form focus groups to confirm their beliefs and to see how buyers will like their product. All fine and good, but also all equally arrogant and introspective.

This approach misses many key considerations. The first and most important is: what market should we be in? What are the strengths we bring to the table? What value can we add to the product to differentiate it? Finally, and equally important, is the question: what will make people buy our offering?

In mature saturated markets, cost is a clear differentiator. To remain viable, companies must be able to change their markets. They must be able to redefine the markets and redifferentiate their products in the new markets. This is not an option; it is an obvious fact and it is basic to survival. It is also a fairly new concept, at least from the standpoint that it has seldom been practiced.

If we assume that price is the big differentiator and that the company must stay in that market, then the company is in real trouble. The costs of everything become the key drivers. This is a declining situation. The market is stable or deteriorating and it will be taken away by a company that is creative enough to change it. In reality there is only so much water that you can squeeze from the turnip before it is drained—if you can squeeze any out at all. Similarly, you can only cut costs so much. Then the product will become unviable and the company will go out of business. So cost is a key factor only in a declining market. If a company is faced with this situation, it must do something or the result will be inevitable.

The only way to break out of this situation is to redefine the market and the only way to do this is through perceived buyer value. The values of the buyer, especially the intangible values, can and must be defined and used to manipulate buying patterns to define a new niche or submarket. There is simply no choice.

Unless companies break the grip in concept that the financial community and the investment community have over them, they will eventually fail. The ability to challenge this assumption is a key first step in creating a sustainable future.

ASSUMPTION 9.3
THE CUSTOMER'S VIEWPOINT IS NOT REALLY AN IMPORTANT FACTOR IN SALES.

Although there is a much greater awareness of the customer and the value of customer loyalty than there was several decades ago, many companies continue to believe that loyalty is not related to value. Thus many businesses continue to operate under a "just good enough" philosophy.

This assumption is often held unconsciously, but there are managers who actually operate on an explicit "just enough" basis. "Spend what is needed to get by or to get just enough support or service." Excess in capability or quality is just a waste. This is clearly a financial perspective. It is also the basis for the ever popular saying, "We need a Chevy solution, not a Cadillac." The basis for this belief is that companies should provide just enough of anything to get by. This is evident in everything these companies do. They build in only enough quality to get by. They build in only enough service, enough advertising to get by. These companies are virtually milking every penny out of every department. Working for such companies is tough and the attitudes of the staff, including the sales and customer services staffs, reflect this. They do just enough to get by. Ergo, the customer is shorted in everything. These companies believe that the only customer value is price: they look at everything in terms of cost and provide the minimum they believe is required. Quality in every sense is kept to a minimum. Customer service is almost nonexistent. The questions to ask to begin challenging this assumption are: is quality really all that important? Is it really of value? Does it differentiate products? Does it really affect your ability to market your products?

Assumption 9.4
Quality is important, but it is not the most important differentiator.

According to experts like Deming and Cosby, quality of goods and services produced by the company is everything. Clearly, quality is a value determinant. Quality must be applied to every aspect of the business. It applies to material as much as it does to product longevity and to customer service. Quality is virtually a chain made of many parts, everything involved in making, providing, and servicing a product. Any link can break the chain. Any break can destroy a customer's confidence and loyalty.

A quality chain should not be confused with a value chain. Quality chains are built by looking at quality, as defined by the value a buyer places on quality for a product and then defining all the components that are involved in providing that level of quality. It is not defined "from the customer in" and it is not defined by engineering. It is defined by a specific value and then it is implemented through a cross-functional look at process. When defined through this process, the importance of quality is not a vague, disassociated guess. It is tied to the customer and it is one of the real differentiators in a market.

In many companies, management has promoted quality. One sees posters and hears managers bragging about how their companies look at quality. Many of these companies do, in fact, try very hard to provide a quality product. However, some do not recognize the reality of a quality chain, so they fail on essential links in the chain. An example is customer service. To cut cost, many companies have cut down their number of customer service representatives. They have also added automated phone systems that really serve as a block to customer access to the service. While this saves staff and cost, it breaks the value chain. If you purchase a product that is good, but you have a question and need assistance, the value of the product shifts from the physical product to the way the company treats you. If you must hang on the phone for a long time you will be frustrated. If you must listen to a long list of automated telephone instructions you will be frustrated. If you then are put on hold again, you will be more frustrated. When you do get through to someone, you are ready to let them know you are frustrated.

After listening to this frustration all day, the customer service representatives are equally surly. The customer doesn't need abruptness. The customer just becomes more frustrated and dissatisfied. If you think they will buy from that company again, ask yourself, would you?

The major taxi cab company in the Chicago suburbs installed an automated phone reservation system. This company was not good at customer service to start with, and this carried over to the implementation of the new phone system. With this system, the customer is forced to key in a great deal of information and then to listen as it is played back. If there is a problem, the customer is asked to hit "O" for the operator. Then it takes up to ten minutes of waiting for the operator to answer. If the customer is curt, the operator mysteriously has an equipment problem and the line is dropped. So the customer learns to be patient or to walk home. Aside from the frustration, one has to wonder whether the people who design systems like this would use them. Consider punching in information from a pay phone in an airport or on the street. Consider pumping in all your change while you wait for an operator and hope that you will be waited on before you run out of quarters. Then consider trying to start all over when your change runs out, your time is used up, and there is still no answer. This company apparently has decided that customer service is not part of quality and not important. Its customer base is not likely to agree.

The assumption that quality is not a key driver in a customer's decision to buy a product can be correct if the product is viewed from a narrow viewpoint. However, when quality is considered a valuable part of every activity of the business, it takes on a very different meaning. If the broader context of a quality chain is accepted, quality becomes a significant factor in gaining and keeping market share. This is true in all markets. The question is one of perspective. If a company can conceive a larger view, it must challenge this assumption.

CHALLENGING ASSUMPTIONS ABOUT BUYER VALUES

Products that are in a mature market have only two options: become competitive based on the lowest price for a given quality, or reposition the product based on a new differentiator—perceived value. Some products will always need to compete on cost and value for the cost. Others can break out of this mold and compete on value to the customer. When management succeeds in repositioning a product, the product behaves like a new offering—it no longer performs or competes like it once did. It essentially gets a new start. All old bets are off.

While this takes creativity, it is possible and many companies are beginning to consider how they can breathe new life into old products. What can they do to update them and reposition them? How can they change them to appeal to a new and maybe younger market? How can the value of a product be improved? What makes it desirable to other market groups? Everything comes down to a few fundamental questions. These are:

1. Is there worthwhile profit in that market?
2. Should we be in that market?
3. Can we reposition and change the market or move to a more profitable market?

These are real unchallenged business assumptions. No one ever questions the need to provide the lowest cost product. Cost is most often considered to be the only buyer value that matters. This assumption can sometimes be wrong.

Value, in terms of the desirable aspects of a product, may be a more important consideration. These buyer values are almost never considered.

We believe that these values are much more important than cost. They define new markets and they are fairly independent of price. In the move to consider the customer, most efforts have focused on how the customer perceives the company and how they interact with it. To offset this problem, a Japanese car manufacturer sent a large group of its staff to Europe to gain an understanding of the market. They talked to people and lived with them. They learned what they considered to be important. They learned about the buyer's perception of value. This understanding of value was brought back to Japan and used to design a new car. Its success was virtually certain, and it did succeed.

The lessons of the past few years clearly show that in value classification, the buyer's perceptions are all that count. The clear message is that if a company wants to understand the buyer, it must go far beyond the normal, sterile focus groups. It must understand how the potential buyers think and what motivates them—the planners, designers, and marketing staffs must understand the buyers' perceived values.

OVERVIEW OF THE VALUE POINT CONCEPT

Perceived value defines any product, service, or job. Whatever is important can be defined and a value provided. Any product will have a given set of assets that are important for each buyer group. This is true for any customer, of any variety.

Each feature of a product is important in determining the buyer group based on the values the group relates to the feature. If the values of the buyer group show the feature is not important, it will not be a differentiator for that group. The important "features" for a given group of buyers are each developed by key actions of the company: "value points." If the value points of the group show the feature is important, it can become a competitive advantage. The key is in finding what is important to the target group. This same key allows a company to move a product from one buyer group to another—based on the perceived value of the feature that will move the product. It is possible to take a tired product in a commodity market and change it to match the value points of a higher market and renew the ability of the product to generate sales.

VALUE EVALUATION USED INTERNALLY

With any activity, internal staff assigns value to change based on personal factors. In changing anything, you must improve the value of the product you are changing to those who will use it or work with it, or it will be of questionable worth. Production input is not the key. Cutting cost is important, but to improve the likelihood of success, cost and ROI should not be used as the only motivating factors in a change. The results of changes driven by financial considerations or technology considerations can be a reduction of staff. Without a reduction in work, the other staff members must now increase effort. The company may seem to win, but the win is temporary. The change will not have provided value from the staff viewpoint. If the staff meets the change with passive resistance, the new operation is not going to succeed. Even if cost was saved, the company will lose in the long run as work quality decreases, absenteeism increases, and customer service decreases. If the response of management continues to represent only financial cuts and does not tie into the staff values, the staff may rise in mutiny, as in a union action, and the company will lose much more: even if they win the battle, they will lose the hearts of the workers and so lose productivity, loyalty, and staff concern in the long run.

In any improvement, the driver must be defined in terms of the company's, the user's, and the staff's value points. While some will argue about the order that these groups are listed in, any change requires the acceptance of all three groups. Value, in these cases, equates to "WIIFMs," or "what's in it for me?" Change must give someone a personally positive result. If any group does not want or like the change, either it will not be implemented or it will fail.

If the customer does not respond to the change, the company will lose market share or go out of business. If the company does not agree with the change, it will be stopped. If the staff does not agree with the change, it will not provide benefits to the customer or the company. If value is a major factor in any change, from the three perspectives, consensus will not be necessary. At least, consensus will not be needed to make decisions and the process of change will be more accurate and be completed much faster.

In focusing work and budget, value points are again the key.

WHAT, WHY, HOW?

Value point focus is also important. Build the needed quality into the things that need quality—based on the perception of value to the user or customer. If longevity is the key, then quality is important. If the product is throw-away cheap, perhaps quality is not important.

VALUE-BASED EVALUATION

Companies have always been trying to understand their financial positions. Various methods of accounting have been tried and none has provided the necessary level of information. Today this continues. Financial information is usually old and often not reliable. It is certainly not the information that is needed to really guide a business. If good, reliable, timely financial information was the key, one would think that better business decisions would be made and that, given the sophistication of our computer systems, the U.S. would not be losing a market war with the rest of the world.

The key indicators of the strength of a business have long been financial. The worth of the company in terms of its stock has been directly tied to the financial reports of the company and its financial actions—like cutting costs. We must propose another set of indicators to add to the financial ones of the past. These indicators relate to the customer and to the customer's perception of value.

The true strength of a company is its ability to bring a high-quality product to market at a price that is acceptable to the customer. There is nothing new in this. The innovation is in using all of these factors to evaluate both operations and market positioning. If we assume that the product is marketable, then we must look at the value that is placed on the product by the customer. The market shows that high-priced radios can sell fine and that they do not compete with low-cost radios when the quality value points of radios are greater.

Value is thus the measure of perceived worth in terms of want, not need. This view of value places customer feelings and beliefs above other indicators—including the financial indicators. The fact is that if perceived value is high enough, there will be a market for the product. But the market will be defined in terms of a product's value to the individual buying group. Experience has clearly proven that need is not the most important factor in determining buying patterns. Customers often pass up what they need to get what they want. Want thus becomes a key driver and it is therefore a large part of the value equation. This fact was proven in the Great Depression, when people seemed to find the money to buy entertainment. It was clearly worth the price to gain diversion and escape the real world for a while.

For the sociologists, let's assume that there is a category of things that must be purchased to take care of our basic needs. The value approach certainly holds true for these items. Even needed products like food are differentiated in terms of value. For example, fresh vegetables cost more than older ones because they offer greater perceived value. The cooked state is the same for both very fresh and older vegetables and the taste is generally considered the same, so why do fresh vegetables cost more? The answer is in the perceived value of fresher vegetables. And perception is the key concept.

In any class of buyers, perception changes constantly. It is influenced by every change around us. This change allows a product to be updated and upgraded and that can open new markets and move products out of basic commodity groupings where the only differentiator is price.

In any market, perceived value can be identified and measured. The value indicators are different in different markets. If we define a market as the buyer group in a given location for a product group and then further break the market down by socioeconomic lines, we find that value for each group defines the perceived values for that product group to the customer group. (The same is true for any service or manufacturing operation.) This layering of values along group lines creates ranges for any grouping of products that define the products' acceptability to the consumer group and what they will pay for it. For example, for many families with moderate incomes a medium-priced car will be thought to offer great value. The more comfort features the better, but they are willing to pay for the ones they want—options. Higher income families look for a very different type of car. Here perceived value is found in image and performance features. The features the moderate income family look for are included and the value of the higher-priced car is provided through a different set of indicators or "wants."

Following this line of reasoning, it is clear that a company has two ways to go in marketing a product. The first is the financial answer: cut costs and reduce price. Only corporate financial values are considered here. This is fine for a saturated market where no changes can improve value. In a market where you can provide additional value, the price is not a real issue. Of course there are reality ranges, but the fact that automobiles are priced from a few thousand to over three-quarters of a million dollars demonstrates that price is not as important as value in that particular market. Realistically, the lower the price the more people can afford the product. However, the reality range varies for product and customer base. Even an old tired product can be improved and marketed in a different reality range when it offers different perceived values.

The key is in defining the value points and then the reality ranges for pricing. Japanese industry has obviously mastered this approach.

ACTIVITY-BASED VS. VALUE-BASED COSTING

Activity-based cost accounting is a potentially great improvement in corporate financial management. Expense money is consumed by process (activity), not by organization. But traditional methods use organization structure to account for expense, and production costs are accounted for empirically using standard costing. Activity-based costing can help management to do a better job of controlling production costs. But again, value is a better indicator.

Any work should add value to a product or service, and the value added should obviously exceed the cost of the work. While this seems utterly basic, much of the trend toward activity-based costing focuses attention on work (activities) that seems to have high costs in relation to other work, ignoring the value added.

Again, cost alone can become a misleading indicator. High cost in an activity area may be quite appropriate, if there is high value being added. High activity cost adding low value is certainly not acceptable, and it is those activities that the process improvement spotlight should seek to expose.

Everything has a value point. It will either be additive (positive), neutral (zero), or minus (negative). Any value point that is zero should be viewed as unnecessary and a review conducted to see if it can be eliminated. The same review should be applied to both low negative and low positive value points. Removing negative value points is the key to improvement.

Each reality group or customer group will have a specific set of value points that defines the group according to what they think is important or has value. When these are different among the interacting groups, as in a change or improvement effort in a company, the change will fail—see Chapter 6, "The Three Views of Business Planning." To have any chance of success, all groups' value points must be defined, agreed upon, and used to align the results to improve the value points of each group. If this is not done, the effort will simply not provide the results that everyone is looking for. If there is enough disconnection in the sets of value points, the effort will not succeed.

USING VALUE POINTS TO CHANGE MARKETING APPROACH

In defining a value point, first define the customer and the market for any product or service. If the product or service is marketable—someone wants to obtain it or use it—then the questions are why and what for? Next look at what the customer perceives as valuable. For example, if longevity of use is the key, then quality is important. If longevity is not expected, then quality is not important. Are additional features or such things as higher-quality metals or plastics in the case or frame important? Are they important enough to make a difference in the product's ability to compete? If they are, then they are value points and they can be used to move a product into a higher reality range.

A product or service only has value with respect to a potential buyer. Therefore, the first step in value point analysis is to establish a buyer matrix for the product or service being evaluated. The matrix has a row for each buyer class and a column for each value indicator. To estimate the measurement of a value, define the indicators, or the characteristics that make a product or service valuable, vis-à-vis a particular sort of buyer. Place the name of each indicator in a row on the top line of a matrix. Then assign to each characteristic, for each buyer:

0 for not wanted or needed,

1 for not very important,

2 for needed, but only marginally wanted,

3 for very important, but only possibly wanted, or

4 for must have, highly desired (can't live without it; world-class)

These numbers can be obtained from market studies or experience. For some products and some services, it will be difficult to even think of differentiators other than price, but these are the best opportunities for creative marketing. A weight must also be assigned to each characteristic, again using 0 to 4, indicating how much influence that particular characteristic generally has on each class of buyers. The difference between the weights and the indicator values is that the weights do not change, while the indicators can be increased by changing how much of that indicator the company can put into the product. For example, current color choice may be a small influence (weight), and may have a small value indication as well, say an influence of 1 and a value of 1. Coming up with a new set of color selections for the product may increase the desirability to a 4, but the influence of color will still be low. When the weight is high and the desirability of the company's product is low, there is obviously a competitive disadvantage. It is usually appropriate to give a low weight to an indicator that is new and uniquely created for the company's product and untested in the market, even if it seems likely to be very advantageous in the market.

Finally, assign a percentage to each class that shows the proportion of buyers in that class. If possible, this should be based on actual product sales records. Here is a sample value-point matrix:

	%	Color Choice	Wt	Quality	Wt	Price	Wt	Safety	Wt
Tots, Male	2%	4	3	2	1	4	4	0	0
Tots, Fem.	1%	4	4	2	0	2	1	0	0
City Folk	40%	2	4	4	3	2	3	4	3
Country Folk	57%	4	4	4	3	4	3	2	1

Now we can look at the opportunity to change the product or service and move it to a less price-sensitive market position. This will be possible if the other (weighted) buyer value factors can be made to outweigh the value increase of a lower price. Price will almost always be a value factor, of course. In addition, the new value profile must be achievable at a cost that will be recovered.

VALUE POINTS APPLIED TO OPERATIONAL DECISIONS

Value points can be used to help make operational decisions. For this purpose, value replaces cost in making a variety of production determinations. Value points can also be used in human resources support. Value can be used to make decisions that can make jobs easier and more rewarding.

Because of the breakdown of employee loyalty (see Chapter 5, "The Human Asset"), the values of workers have become selfish. Few employees really focus on what is good for their company. They assume the company will stay in business or else they leave it. So the good of the company is a distant issue to many, including managers. The two areas of values, personal and corporate, do overlap at values related to making the job easier and in building a good product. Cutting costs is related to a set of company values that most workers have learned to ignore—if they do make an improvement and cut costs someone will lose their job. Not much incentive. However, establishing a value system that is acceptable to everyone can provide considerable benefits.

People bring their value systems with them. They cannot be separated at work or in their personal lives. These value systems are complex, but they can be defined and measured in terms of specific actions, subassembly parts, quality, or almost anything.

The question is how to focus on the values applicable to the operations situation, the product being made, or the service being rendered. The standard approach to managing a business uses two very different sets of numerical systems. These are market analysis and financial/budget review. Both are kept separate and they are seldom viewed as part of a composite whole. Value points apply to both. After value points are identified, they are cross-indexed to three management tools:

1. the budget;
2. marketing reports and studies; and
3. the process map that shows workflow in each department.

Changing one of the factors shown in any of these tools ripples throughout the entire company. The ripple effect of this will apply to the entire manufacturing operation and to the business operation that runs the company. For example, a great product with a poor customer service group will produce many negative value points. Not only is the customer service value point low, but the production operation is also lowered by poor customer service. The same is true for support areas, such as accounting. If customers have questions and cannot talk to anyone because all they get is voice mail and no one returns their calls, accounting will be a negative value point, and it will influence customer service, which will be the next group the customers call.

Success for the company and for each of its products and services can only be achieved in the long term when all the value points are positive. If a value point is evaluated and found to need improvement, it is a negative factor.

Operational analysis using value points begins by identifying the points in the process where value is added. These points can cover a broad operation (like customer service) or they can be very detailed. For each point, the value is determined by adding the value that the point adds directly to each product or service that it actually deals with, and then adding the value it supplies to other value points. Finally, the value that it obtains from other services is subtracted. The sum is divided by the cost of the value point. This analysis can either use a real dollar scale or it can use any consistent artificial scale. A formula for the mathematically inclined to determine the score of a single value point is:

$$P_1 = \frac{v_1 + \sum\limits_{i=2}^{n} g - \sum\limits_{j=2}^{m} t}{c_1}$$

where P_1 = the score for the first value point, v_1 = the value added of the first value point, g_i = the value given by the first value point to the ith value point, t_j = the value the first value point takes from the jth value point, and c_1 = the cost of the first value point. These scores can be used in a variety of ways, alone or in conjunction with the marketing tables described above. The simplest way is to find the activities with the highest and lowest scores and just find out why they are as they are.

Just considering the concept of value replacing cost as the principal approach to evaluating business activities will start any company toward increased management control. The first step is challenging the hidden assumption that cost is the only controllable variable in producing goods and services. The second step is to stop using cost as the principal indicator of operational efficiency. Just don't do it.

THE MANAGER OF
THE FUTURE

The manager of the future will have more, not fewer, hidden assumptions to deal with. Business will become more complex as it absorbs more technology and becomes more globalized. The manager will be working harder and probably getting less satisfaction out of it. In some ways, it is a grim picture. But competition will see to it that the survivors are better managers than business is now accustomed to.

The future begins now, so there must be some forward-thinking managers today who are the precursors of managers to come. Indeed, there are such people. Some of them gained their special skills of necessity, being more deeply immersed in international, electronic, and supercompetitive business situations than most. There is an especially good chance that managers with professional backgrounds in the three major aspects of large company work already have the traits of the next century. These three types of big business work are operations, technology, and accounting. Any senior business person who has been successful in all three areas has most of the skills of tomorrow.

BUSINESS 2000

What are the major differences that can be expected in business in the next century? While we cannot be sure of the directions that technology and chance will take, we can predict some things with a high level of confidence. Here are only three examples of what will be the key trends of future business:

Speed—Companies that can move quickly will survive; the others will not. This trait goes under various names, like "the nimble company" and "change-readiness." It is a difficult capability to achieve, since it requires that management have full control over every aspect of the company and that the company's employees trust management to implement change without inflicting damage on the workers. It is generally known that speed will be increasingly required to respond to the rapid changes in almost every market. However, the requirement to respond to brand new business opportunities may be even more important. Imagine that you have just unexpectedly received the patent rights to a teleportation machine that works. Your contract with the inventor requires cash flow starting in 30 days or the rights will be revoked. What do you do?

Flexibility—Another obvious capability? Not quite: flexibility in the future will mean not only that companies will be doing a greater variety of work, but that some of the work will be new, or will be shifted back and forth based on the change of a microscopic cost element. For example, companies will be taking parts of many operations considered core business today and farming them out. The same companies might discover there are cost advantages in doing some other things and may take in outside, perhaps even a competitor's, work. These changes will require either having no permanent workforce or having one that can do anything. Flexibility will also mean the ability to buy and sell parts of the company every day or so. Office space is already being redefined: some companies are no longer assigning permanent offices. The next step is that having offices, or even factories, may become obsolete. Flexibility really means coming up with new ways to do business on the fly, implementing them, and then changing them or selling them off faster than ink could dry in 1950.

Narrow Margins—There will be much smaller profits in the future. Profits will fall, victims of competition. To survive narrow margins, companies will be forced to rely upon volume sales of more products and services than today. This factor also implies the ability to predict costs and values with much more accuracy than is common today. Balancing costs and revenues will be an even bigger part of the future manager's job than it is today.

How will managers work in all of this continual and rapid movement? Some will flourish. Others will not be able to survive. There will be very little middle ground. And how much room for hidden assumptions will there be in companies of the future? None whatever. Every detail of every business transaction will be based on analysis and decisions.

THE RENASCENCE MANAGER

The world seems to move faster every day. An industrial or financial manager of the 1940s would not only be at a disadvantage doing business now, but would also not like the change. There are some agreeable aspects to today's business climate, but there is also more individual competition for fewer jobs and the work is just plain harder. Likewise, the enthusiasm over the dawn of the information age is hard to explain when it is examined from the viewpoint of the quality of business life. The industrial revolution was not pleasant for most of those who were caught up in it, and the information-based society may be accompanied by a whole new set of troubles.

Business is just now catching up to where the rest of society has been for some time. The technology revolution we are in now started with the telephone, automobile, and airplane in the early 1900s. Most managers use all three of those inventions more often than they would choose to. But most business people did not feel the pressures of technology until they resulted in the global competition that threatens every job. Society at large has been much more affected.

Society has reacted in many ways to the great change of pace that this century brought with it. Most new inventions are welcomed with open arms, without regard for the problems that might come with them. No one, however, was completely unaware that social pressures were on the rise. In 1917, the American poet Edna St. Vincent Millay published her famous *Renascence*, in which she wrote:

> *But East and West will pinch the heart*
> *That cannot keep them pushed apart;*
> *And he whose soul is flat—the sky*
> *Will cave in on him by and by.*

Millay thus recommended heart and soul as the keys to survival during the new age she was living in. What about management? Heart and soul are not what a manager needs to survive. Much more sophisticated tools will be required in our new business age.

THE FUTURE MANAGER'S TOOL BAG

Managers of the future will probably come out of school better equipped than today's graduates. They will have a number of new capabilities, right out of the classroom. A few of these will give them the abilities that will differentiate them from today's business people:

Special Knowledge—The general manager of the past is already giving way to more specialization in the ranks of management. Schools have been slow to adapt to this trend, not many offering any really specialized training, such as engineering management, managing financial services (as opposed to financial management), and managing technology. This will change and it will offer significant advantages.

Special Tools—Spreadsheets are very powerful, but there are other areas into which the computer will intrude shortly, such as process optimization systems and business models. However, it is not so much the tools that will be different, but the abilities to use them. Today only a handful of senior managers can use a spreadsheet. Most CEOs have difficulty with electronic mail. The business world of the future will move too quickly to allow anyone without a highly developed technology capability to even participate.

Luck—Every future manager needs luck, especially to get that first job; that is very difficult even today.

Luck is always helpful. Perhaps luck will be more important in the next century when even conservative ventures will have much higher failure rates than risky ones have today. But tomorrow as today, no manager will be able to rely upon luck. Just don't do it.

INDEX

About the Authors

Joel Brandon and Daniel Morris are principals of Morris, Tokarski, Brandon and Company (MTB), a consulting firm that specializes in business process improvement and change management. MTB is the creator of the Positioning and Re-engineering system (PARs), the first computer program specifically intended for business re-engineering. Re-engineering is the most notorious of the trendy approaches whose flaws and erroneous assumptions are examined in *Just Don't Do It!* The authors' clients have included AMOCO, KRAFT, Empire Blue Cross/Blue Shield, The World Bank, NASA, UNISYS, Siemans AT, Commerce Clearing House, and many others. Before forming their consultancy, Brandon and Morris held senior management positions with large corporations and in government. They are the authors of *Re-engineering Your Business* and *Relational Systems Development*, both published by McGraw-Hill.